ALSO BY ARTHUR ASHE

Days of Grace
A Hard Road to Glory
Off the Court
Arthur Ashe's Tennis Clinic
Portrait in Motion

ALSO BY ALEXANDER McNAB

The Tennis Doctor

Arthur Ashe on Tennis

ARTHUR ASHE
ON TENNIS

Strokes, Strategy,
Traditions, Players, Psychology,
and Wisdom

ARTHUR ASHE

with Alexander McNab

Alfred A. Knopf   New York   1995

THIS IS A BORZOI BOOK
PUBLISHED BY ALFRED A. KNOPF, INC.

Library of Congress Cataloging-in-Publication Data
Ashe, Arthur.
Arthur Ashe on tennis : strokes, strategy, traditions, players,
psychology, and wisdom / Arthur Ashe with Alexander McNab. — 1st ed.
p.   cm.
ISBN 0-679-43797-5
1. Tennis.   I. McNab, Alexander.   II. Title.
GV995.A75   1995
796.342—dc20   94-29542   CIP

Manufactured in the United States of America

FIRST EDITION

Contents

Contents

STRATEGY

TRADITIONS

PLAYERS

Acknowledgments

Three individuals were instrumental in seeing this project of Arthur's through to completion: Peter Sawyer of the Fifi Oscard Agency, Arthur's longtime literary representative; Jonathan Segal of Alfred A. Knopf, who edited the book; and Jeanne Moutoussamy-Ashe. Thanks, too, to Donna Doherty, our editor at *Tennis* magazine.

Foreword

The idea of writing this book occurred to Arthur Ashe as we were walking down a fairway on the East Course of the Winged Foot Golf Club in Mamaroneck, New York, in the fall of 1990. One member of our group was Frank Hannigan, the former executive director of the U.S. Golf Association and, like Arthur, an analyst for ABC Sports. Arthur had just responded to a couple of Hannigan's questions about *Levels of the Game,* John McPhee's book about Arthur and Clark Graebner and their 1968 semifinal match at the U.S. Open.

When he had finished answering Hannigan, Arthur turned to me, his instruction-writing collaborator for eleven years at *Tennis* magazine, and said, "We ought to do a book."

Our original notion was for Arthur to answer the most frequent questions he was asked about tennis. We did hours of interviews for the book in late 1991 and early 1992 and started writing chapters. He then began work on his memoir, *Days of Grace.* But he never stopped thinking about this book. He kept polishing the material. The last time we spoke he reiterated his intention, once *Days of Grace* was done, to complete work on this book and his desire to see it published.

In retirement, Arthur stayed current with the game, not only through his work with ABC, HBO, and tennis equipment companies, but also through direct observation. He was a habitué of the outside courts in the early days of Wimbledon and the French and U.S. Opens, where he would check out the latest phenoms. He would scout the juniors during the Easter Bowl tournament at the Doral in Miami. He would stay in touch with his former playing companions who had moved into pro coaching, such as Stan Smith and Brian Gottfried. He would consult with the game's sages, such as Pancho Segura. And he would pick the brains of innovators in the teaching business, such as sports psychologist Jim Loehr, biomechanist Jack Groppel, and master teaching pros Vic Braden and Dennis Van der Meer.

As a tennis teacher himself, Ashe preached what today would be called a classic game—smooth, no-frills strokes, including a one-handed backhand. The fundamentals of his generation remained his prescription for club players even in the 1990s. However, he recognized that there was more than one way to hit a ball, and he was an expert at drawing lessons for club players from the more unorthodox and flamboyant styles of the pros.

The wisest and most moving tennis lesson I heard Arthur give, though, was not in response to an inquiry about the game. It was in response to an inquiry about how he managed to turn the many negative medical challenges in his life—his heart attacks, his bypass operations, and his battle with AIDS—into energizing, positive crusades. His reply: "A competitive athlete never gives up. He may run out of time, but he never gives up." It is an attitude that can make us all not only better players but better human beings as well.

Alexander McNab
Fairfield, Connecticut
July 1994

INTRODUCTIONS

ARTHUR ASHE REMEMBERED
by John McPhee

He once described his life as "a succession of fortunate circumstances." He was in his twenties then. More than half of his life was behind him. His memory of his mother was confined to a single image: in a blue corduroy bathrobe she stood in a doorway looking out on the courts and playing fields surrounding their house, which stood in the center of a Richmond playground. Weakened by illness, she was taken to a hospital that day, and died at the age of twenty-seven. He was six.

It was to be his tragedy, as the world knows, that he would leave his own child when she was six, that his life would be trapped in a medical irony as a result of early heart disease, and death would come to him prematurely, as it had to his mother.

His mother was tall, with long soft hair and a face that was gentle and thin. She read a lot. She read a lot to him. His father said of her, "She was just like Arthur Junior. She never argued. She was quiet, easygoing, kindhearted."

If by legacy her son never argued, he was also schooled, instructed, coached not to argue, and as he moved alone into alien country he fashioned not-arguing into an enigma and turned the enigma into a weapon. When things got tough (as

I noted in the book *Levels of the Game* twenty-six years ago), he had control. Even in very tight moments, other players thought he was toying with them. They rarely knew what he was thinking. They could not tell if he was angry. It was maddening, sometimes, to play against him. Never less than candid, he said that what he liked best about himself on a tennis court was his demeanor: "What it is is controlled cool, in a way. Always have the situation under control, even if losing. Never betray an inward sense of defeat."

And of course he never did—not in the height of his athletic power, not in the statesmanship of the years that followed, and not in the endgame of his existence. If you wished to choose a single image, you would see him standing there in his twenties, his lithe body a braid of cables, his energy without apparent limit, in a court situation indescribably bad, and all he does is put his index finger on the bridge of his glasses and push them back up the bridge of his nose. In the shadow of disaster, he hits out. Faced with a choice between a conservative, percentage return or a one-in-ten flat-out blast, he chooses the blast. In a signature manner, he extends his left arm to point upward at lobs as they fall toward him. His overheads, in fire bursts, put them away. His backhand is, if anything, stronger than his forehand, and his shots from either side for the most part are explosions. In motions graceful and decisive, though, and with reactions as fast as the imagination, he is a master of drop shots, of cat-and-mouse, of miscellaneous dinks and chips and (riskiest of all) the crosscourt half volley. Other tennis players might be wondering who in his right mind would attempt something like that, but that is how Ashe plays the game: at the tensest moment, he goes for the all but impossible. He is predictably unpredictable. He is unreadable. His ballistic serves move in odd patterns and come off the court in unexpected ways. Behind his impassive face—behind the enigmatic glasses, the lifted chin, the first-mate-on-the-bridge look—there seems to be, even from this distance, a smile.

THE PLAYER

by Billie Jean King

Arthur Ashe motivated. He taught. We listened when he spoke. He used tennis for a greater good. Many players don't. He made a difference.

Even during his playing days, Arthur wasn't narrowly focused on tennis, like so many of today's young players are. He wasn't just a tennis player. He was always searching and always thinking. He had other things going on in that head of his, things he cared about or wanted to accomplish.

As I said at his memorial service in 1993, working at HBO on its Wimbledon coverage was a great gift, because I finally got to know Arthur. There was so much more there than the cool exterior he presented on the tennis court. There was warmth, passion, intelligence, and love.

Arthur and I were born the same year, 1943. I first read stories about him when he was in St. Louis, where he spent his senior year of high school so he could play winter tennis on the indoor courts there. The stories described his Richmond, Virginia, background and his coach, Dr. Robert Walter Johnson. He then came to southern California—where I grew up—to play at UCLA, for whom he won the NCAA singles and doubles titles in 1965. In those years, he and his UCLA teammate Charlie Pasarell would show up at the

Westbury Hotel in London just before Wimbledon, having flown in from playing in the NCAA tournament. That was a fairly normal occurrence—flying in to play Wimbledon with only a couple of days to practice on grass courts. No one questioned it. Nowadays, it's different—players of their calibre aren't in college, and they have ample preparation for Wimbledon.

Arthur's tennis game at times was explosive. Both his serve and his backhand were truly beautiful strokes. The rhythm on his serve was wonderful, and the footwork he used on it was unusual: he would take a step back and then glide up to the line as he swung.

Like many players of our generation, he had a dodgy forehand: his was a pretty wristy Continental stroke, hit with a straight arm. Maybe our forehands weren't better because we didn't have anyone to mimic. When we started playing tennis, there weren't any great forehands around. The best players of the 1950s, such as Ken Rosewall and Darlene Hard, had far better backhands. We didn't see good forehands until much later. We were emulating ordinary shotmaking. Once a good stroke comes around, you emulate it, or you create a great shot yourself and then everyone emulates you. Arthur also had a hard time getting down on low forehand volleys. Years later, he would say with good humor, "Ah, I couldn't bend my knees."

During the time Arthur broke through and won the first U.S. Open as an amateur in 1968, he and his U.S. Davis Cup teammates were very aloof toward us women players. The men were polite, but there was no way you could get close to them because they wouldn't hit with you. The Australians, Rod Laver, Roy Emerson, and Fred Stolle, would hit with us every day; odd when you think about it, because Australians are supposed to be more chauvinistic.

Indeed, for a long time Arthur was worrying almost only about men's tennis. Except for his interest in the black women players such as Zina Garrison and Lori McNeil, who meant a lot to him, he didn't seem to care that much about women's tennis or women's sports or helping women. That was until his wife, Jeanne, came into his life. After she encouraged him to attend a Women's Sports Foundation press conference, he became enormously supportive. Then, of course, when his daughter, Camera, came along, she put him over the top. He now had a daughter, and he wanted her to have all of the opportunities boys had. That helped our relationship, because he saw me in a different light. I had always been trying to help get opportunities for girls as well as boys, and all of a sudden that made much more sense to him.

Our career paths on the court crossed most prominently in 1975 at Wimbledon. Watching him win the men's singles title the day after I won the women's was special because his demeanor and body language were *expressive.* After winning match point against Jimmy Connors, he turned around, looked up at the competitors' box, and raised his fist to his friend and advisor, Donald Dell. It was the first time most of the world saw Arthur show some of his true emotional self. I don't think he liked Connors at all.

The most wonderful thing is that Arthur won that match playing against the grain of what he had always done, which was to hit the ball hard and hit it flat. Instead, he left his comfort zone, went to plan B and hit wide slice serves that made Connors fully extend on his two-handed backhand, and chipped low to Jimmy's forehand. Playing what you would consider a plan B is not an easy task for a player in those circumstances, the Wimbledon final. It was a great match not only because Arthur beat somebody he truly wanted to beat, and beat him badly, but because of the *way* he did it.

Arthur had a reverence and love for Wimbledon. One year he brought Camera there. He took her hand and they walked around the grounds as he talked about different matches on each court, about his memories and the importance of the place. Even though he knew she probably wouldn't remember much of it, he said it was important to do, especially for him. It was a way for him to pass his story to the next generation.

We still have a lot of "Arthur moments" at HBO. One happened in 1994, when Lori McNeil beat Steffi Graf in the first round of Wimbledon and went all the way to the semifinals. Arthur used to root for Lori so much. Finally here she was starting to show some of the potential that God gave her, and Arthur wasn't there to share in it. Jim Lampley, our host at Wimbledon, was overcome with emotion when he thought about Arthur after Lori upset Steffi.

Arthur loved to theorize that only the tall men, players six feet one or more, can win Wimbledon now. The big servers, with their height and today's powerful racquets, were the only ones who were going to win. Tennis was going to be less and less a small man's game.

We often discussed how to help the game grow. Maybe we approached it through different means, but our goals were totally in tune: How can we help this game of ours? How can we help minorities get involved? Tennis is quite small. We would always think about how many people we have lost from the sport, and how many people never even had an interest in it piqued, because tennis is not hospitable enough.

Arthur also talked about his early days, when he couldn't enter tournaments because of his color. He spoke of how difficult it was not to be accepted, not to be allowed to play, because he was good enough to be on the court with the other players. He was raised to act in a manner that was beyond reproach—don't rock the boat, just do your best. Because of the way he was brought up, and because of society's restraints, he was never allowed to have the freedom of expression on the court that others had.

He was very envious of John McEnroe, although he used to become angry with McEnroe when Arthur was captain of the U.S. Davis Cup team and McEnroe was its star. Arthur had to be the perfect guy out there, suck it up, and never say a word, and here McEnroe would lose his lid and get away with it. But even McEnroe's behavior could not dampen Arthur's love of Davis Cup. And in a pleasant irony, McEnroe later assumed the position of chairman of Arthur's Safe Passage Foundation, an organization that gets inner-city children involved in tennis as a way of teaching them sportsmanship, discipline, and other important precepts of life.

Arthur, like Bjorn Borg and Chris Evert, was a low-arousal champion, whereas Connors, McEnroe, and I were very high-arousal champions. But you have to appreciate each other and celebrate each other's differences. Still, many times, Arthur deep down was smoldering. You could see it in his jawline. He would start to get that look, and you would know that Arthur was feeling a lot but not expressing it in his body language, except for his locked jaw.

In fact, Arthur's passion, which was so restrained on the court, came through in all the causes he fought for, whether it was the fight against apartheid, his advocacy regarding Haiti, or helping AIDS research and education.

For example, Ilana Kloss, a former South African player, is absolutely convinced that the changes in her country would not have happened as quickly if Arthur had not played there in the early 1970s. She called Jeanne the day of the South African election in 1994 to tell her so. Arthur, Ilana said, made *that* much of a difference when he went to South Africa because people liked him, in no small part because he was a sportsman. He effected real change in the minds of people not only in South Africa but also in the United States and the rest of the world.

Arthur brought so much to the world beyond tennis, and he did so with grace and dignity. That's what made him who he was.

THE COMPETITOR

by George Vecsey

It was never easy, being Arthur Ashe. He was blessed with high aptitudes and saddled with high expectations, and in a certain kind of young person, that can lead to fractiousness. There is, in prodigies, an inclination to test the boundaries, to see what they can get away with.

In his early days, the only place Arthur felt free enough to improvise, to test his youthful creativity and curiosity, was in the middle of matches, to the befuddlement of his opponents and the disdain of tennis purists. Arthur went for winners more often than was deemed judicious. His independence was often interpreted as a racial characteristic—the inability of an outsider to discipline himself—but in fact it was about genius, about discovery.

Arthur was not a rebel in his daily life. His father, a rather remarkable individualist who built his own world between the insane rigidities of white southern segregation and the tight practicalities of black southern survivalism, taught him very well not to take chances, physically or psychically. And Arthur was taken in, as a tennis and community project, by a series of admirably controlling black mentors.

It could not have been easy for a young man of quick mind and normal appetites to have to live by all these rules. Somebody always wanted something from Arthur Ashe. I gained a singular insight into this when I was a young reporter, just a few years older than Arthur, sometime in the mid-sixties. My paper sent me out to the Nationals at Forest Hills, and I decided to write about the first significant black male tennis player the United States had produced. Not exactly a new idea by then, but what did I know?

Spotting Arthur strolling the narrow lanes of the West Side Tennis Club, carrying a few racquets, I introduced myself and said I wanted to interview him.

"Well, I'd like to do that," is the way I remember his answer, over the decades, "but I'm rather busy right now."

Years and years later, I have often wondered what kind of brutal response John McEnroe or Jimmy Connors would have given in the same context. Arthur Ashe, I realized much later, had been carrying his own racquets out to center court, where he was about to play a match in front of thousands of spectators. Rather busy, indeed.

The only place Arthur was free of parental restrictions, mentor advice, societal pressure, and journalistic intrusion was the tennis court. There he was free to do as he pleased. What were they going to do, stop the match and bellow through a bullhorn, "Arthur, please play the percentages! Arthur, stop aiming for winners all the time! Arthur, enough with the drop shots!"

Those were the days when tennis players were not surrounded by a retinue of bodyguards, advisors, gurus, backhand coaches, forehand coaches, dieticians, strategists, foreign-policy formulators, travel agents, factotums, majordomos, meditation specialists, best friends, agents, managers, parents, siblings, jugglers, and clowns. Players just rather went out and played, as bizarre as that may seem.

Sometimes Arthur played haphazardly. He had the reputation for, how shall we say this, tightening up in close matches. Anybody born in Richmond, Virginia, in 1943, who made it to national tournaments and country clubs during the Bull Connor Years, could hardly have lacked in courage. But sometimes his imagination and his vision kicked in at the wrong time: "Hey, I'm playing badly, and I could get my butt whipped right here. I'd better do something spectacular to save myself." And sometimes his muscles and his mind would lock, and he would lose.

His opponents knew it. There is no better document of this than the classic book *Levels of the Game,* by John McPhee, based on the 1968 semifinals of what was, by then, the United States Open. In that match, Clark Graebner (white, privileged, suburban) waited for a loss of poise from Arthur (black, bootstrapper, southern).

"He's not a steady player," Graebner said about Arthur. "He's a wristy slapper. Sometimes he doesn't even know where the ball is going. He's carefree, lacksadaisical, forgetful. His mind wanders. I've never seen Arthur really discipline himself. He plays the game with the lacksadaisical, haphazard mannerisms of a liberal. He's an underprivileged type who worked his way up."

Nowadays, a diatribe like that would get Graebner in trouble with the Political Correctness Police, but back then, Graebner was merely representing his class. Arthur's response to that characterization probably would have been, "Clark, the word is 'lackadaisical.'" Arthur was always big on improving other people's word power.

Arthur won that semifinal on superior skills and superior heart and superior knowledge. He won the Open final, too, and then he turned professional.

Seven years after the Graebner match, Arthur played what will always be his signature match—the 1975 Wimbledon final. His opponent was young Jimmy Connors, mean and lean, who not only liked to beat opponents, but liked to torment them, pull the wings off flies.

Arthur was already thirty-one years old in 1975, still living down his reputation for smoothness and cool. He consulted two allies of his—Donald Dell, a former player turned agent, and Dennis Ralston, his Davis Cup captain—for advice on how to play Connors. They all understood that you could not merely play Young Jimbo; you had to play with him.

Style points did not count against Connors. Arthur committed himself to a strategy of keeping Connors off balance, hitting soft chip shots wide to his forehand, moving the ball around, not letting Connors get into the match. This required patience and placement, required giving up some flair. (Everything is relative, of course. No tennis player gets to that exalted level without understanding pace and variety, without having an arsenal of strokes and strategy.)

Playing on the legendary Centre Court at Wimbledon, they started by holding serve. But in the third game, while trailing 40–15, Arthur chipped a return to Connors's forehand that threw Connors off balance. Arthur proceeded to stun Connors by breaking him in that third game with varied shots, all over the court. Before a stunned Connors could regroup, he had lost two straight 6–1 sets.

Using all his old shock techniques—muttering to himself, whacking himself with his racquet, working himself into a rage—Connors began charging Arthur's chips and ground strokes, and won the third set 7–5. Then Connors broke Arthur to take a 3–0 lead in the fourth set. Age and form and ranking and momentum were all in Connors's favor.

But Arthur found other strokes to confuse Connors. Arthur rarely lobbed the ball, but in the fifth game he lobbed over Connors to set up a break. And in the ninth game, he broke Connors again, this time with a down-the-line back-hand and a crosscourt backhand that were more like the flamboyant Arthur Ashe. Serving wide to Connors's backhand, Arthur set up Connors for the winning forehand volley. Arthur later said his victory was "destiny," and maybe it was, but only after he had put together a Wimbledon final unlike any match he had ever played.

By now, he was an elder statesman, fully involved in dozens of dreams and projects. The onetime "wristy slapper" had one last great month, January of 1979. Having slipped to No. 257 in the rankings less than a year earlier, Arthur reached the finals of the Grand Prix Masters in Madison Square Garden, and even had two match points against young John McEnroe, before losing.

The next week, at the U.S. Pro Indoor Championships at the Spectrum in Philadelphia, strutting young Vitas Gerulaitis won the first two sets of the semifinal and was serving for the match at 5–4. But Arthur scrambled with an overhead and two soft passing shots, and then placed a backhand past the charging Gerulaitis to break him. Arthur wound up winning the tiebreak, and before Gerulaitis could clear his head, the old man survived four break points in the fifth set to win the match.

After that three-and-a-half-hour match, Arthur wound up losing to Connors in the finals, but it was a great way to go.

"I felt like somebody beat me with a stick," he said afterward. "Not Jimmy—I mean, my body feels like it."

His body was, in fact, breaking down. Six months later, Arthur Ashe would suffer the heart attack that would lead directly to his death from AIDS in 1993. He would be eulogized as an American treasure, mourned for his wisdom and his dedication. It is also part of the Arthur Ashe legacy that this bright young man was once able to experiment, out on the court, where nobody could stop him.

THE LEGACY

by Lori McNeil

It was seemingly an ordinary day in the autumn of 1973. Maybe it would have gone unremembered had things in my life not unfolded as they have. Billie Jean King was playing Bobby Riggs. It was a critical time in her career, a pivotal time in women's professional tennis, and a time I will always use to reference the change in my life. That important match took place in Houston, and though I was born in San Diego, Houston was to be my new home.

Profoundly shy, I was somewhat anxious about moving to a new city. After all, I was only eleven years old and I was leaving behind all that was familiar. Attempting to cheer me, my mother discovered a junior tennis program at MacGregor Park. It was run by a young black man who had made tennis his life, if not his religion. He had a fervor and a devotion to tennis that could be matched only by the one I would later learn was his "true master." There was no better disciple than John Wilkerson, who, with great devotion, attempted to disseminate the message of the master at an inner-city park in Texas.

I found myself immersed in tennis. John not only loved the game, he lived the game. It was his life, and as junior disciples it was to become our life as well. There was no experience that did not relate to tennis, no conversation that did not come back to tennis. Tennis was used as a parable for life. If something went wrong, there was a tennis lesson to be found in the occurrence. Tennis and life were one and the same. We were to be faithful, devoted, fervent, and fearless—a tall order, but our goal nonetheless. And to achieve it, we were to imitate and emulate our master, Arthur Ashe.

At first we took a somewhat naive and simplistic approach by wearing the same shell necklace Arthur always wore around his neck. We were die-hard fans, and with the vividness of our youthful imaginations, we made constant reference to what Arthur would say and what Arthur would do.

We had found in him a mentor. I attempted seriously to walk the walk and talk the talk. Soon it took no effort. I was a believer.

Not long after my conversion, Arthur played a match at River Oaks in Houston. He took that opportunity to visit MacGregor Park. Needless to say, all of us were excited. We were especially scrubbed in our tennis whites. We wanted our appearance to match his meticulous style.

My history as a tennis player began on that day. It did not begin with Rod Laver or Kenny Rosewall, as has the history of so many other professional tennis players. It began with Arthur Ashe.

Arthur fed balls to everybody. I never got to hit with him after I learned to play, because once I got on the tour, he had had his bypass operations and wasn't playing. But that day in 1975 was a thrilling moment for me. Today, it would be like being at a basketball camp and getting a shooting lesson from Michael Jordan.

I remember thinking Arthur was so handsome. He was slim and bronze and scrubbed, and I thought, "No wonder we have chosen him. He is like a god." Our reverence, though, was perhaps not totally by choice, since we had so little choice. Perhaps he was our master simply because we were so darn proud that he was a black man in a sport that involved few, if any, blacks. Consequently, in our program, whether we were male or female, Arthur was our role model.

Later that summer we watched Wimbledon on television. Arthur was playing Jimmy Connors, the world's greatest, in the final. Although Arthur already had become the first and only black man ever to win a Grand Slam tournament, having won the U.S. and Australian Opens earlier in his career, no black man had ever reached the final of Wimbledon. He walked out onto the court, cool and controlled. He seemed unshaken. Deliberately and with great control, he went about his work. He worked hard and he won. The image of him holding the cup of triumph over his head that day will forever be vivid in my mind.

Because I was just learning the game then, I wasn't totally aware of the strategy Arthur used to beat Connors that day. A couple of years ago, though, I watched some film of Arthur playing at his peak. He had a great serve and a great over-head, and I liked his volleys. He played a very clean game, very simple. For instance, he had a very flat forehand, not a lot of topspin. I think I play a lot like that. I can identify with his game.

Unlike Arthur, I have a bad temper, although I have learned to control it, and I'm getting better at doing so. It is amazing how he stayed so cool. I never asked him many questions, but if I could ask him one now, I would say, "How did you do it? When you have hit a terrible shot, how do you just take a deep breath and go on?" My insides churn when that happens. I want to throw my racquet over the fence.

I realize now that the reason John considered Arthur the master of the game was not because he had mastered tennis, but because he had mastered the greatest challenge that life has to offer: he had mastered himself. His conscious mind seemed to control his subconscious, and therefore he had mastered his fears and emotions.

I usually saw Arthur at Wimbledon and the U.S. Open. We went to dinner several times over the years, times at which he would give me his thoughts about my game and offer a bit of advice on what he thought I should do to improve. When my effort paid off at the Virginia Slims Championships at Madison Square Garden in 1992, where I beat Steffi Graf, he was there to say, "Well done," and to remind me to "just keep working hard. Always give your best." Those simple but heartfelt remarks stay with me. Memories of Arthur surfaced when I beat Graf in the first round of Wimbledon in 1994, because it happened on the same Centre Court where he had played that match I watched in 1975.

I have a better insight about my profession from knowing Arthur. When you win Grand Slam tournaments, you have to take on a lot of responsibilities. Arthur had many more responsibilities after winning the U.S. Open and Wimbledon.

And he seemed to balance it all so well. We all aspire to win the Grand Slams of our unique lives. Although our victories seem to be isolated acts, perhaps they are the gift we are given when we remain faithful to the process, the long, laborious process of conquering our most formidable opponent, ourselves.

There is a gap between my career and Arthur's, but to remember meeting him when I was a beginner and now to be doing basically what he did, playing professionally on the tour, is like realizing a dream.

Arthur changed tennis. He gave hope to a group of players who had no spark to ignite the flame that must burn inside if dreams are to come true. It is quite amazing how such a controlled man who displayed so little passion was able to ignite such fire and zeal.

Arthur Ashe was focused and single-minded. He was patient and resolute, but most of all, he was faithful, faithful to the process, even in life's most difficult times. He was willing to work hard. He was willing to fight the good fight. I suppose he had the courage to lose, because I know he had the conviction to win. He succeeded. He conquered himself. And for that, he leaves a legacy of courage to which we all can relate.

Arthur Ashe on Tennis

STROKES

Role Models

As you watch the world's best pros, you must realize that at their level, they often don't do things by the book. They have talent, training, and experience that enable them to break the rules of conventional tennis technique and still succeed. If you try to copy everything they do, you will almost certainly be doomed to frustration.

The new stroking orthodoxy seems to be to do whatever you can to get the job done. But even when you look at the new approaches to playing, with Western grips, two-handed backhands, and larger racquets, when it comes to making contact with the ball, the same principles that applied twenty years ago apply today. If you were to take high-speed pictures of the racquet making contact with the ball, they wouldn't be any different.

I certainly would not advise you to copy Jim Courier. I would not advise you to copy Monica Seles. I used to point to someone like Chris Evert as the best person to copy; now I would suggest emulating Pete Sampras or Mary Joe Fernandez. I would prefer not to teach the two-handed backhand, because it can be a limiting stroke, but I am willing to make exceptions when it is the most practical way for developing players to succeed.

Tailor Your Game to Your Size

One factor in deciding what style of play is best for you is your size.

If you are short, you might be best off adopting a counter-punching style because you won't be able to generate your own power as well as taller players can. You need a consistent, deep first serve, an aggressive return of serve that negates the bigger server's weapon, steady ground strokes (hit the ball high over the net for safety), accurate passing shots, a good lob, and a willingness to keep the point going until you get an opening you can exploit or your opponent makes an error. Attitude counts, too. Nobody likes to play a feisty fighter who will knock down walls to win a match.

If you are tall, use your natural advantage by developing an attacking style. Use the extra leverage and angle you have on the serve by tossing the ball out in front and swinging smoothly. Go to the net, where your imposing figure will make it hard for your opponent to pass and lob you successfully. Use a one-handed backhand to take greater advantage of your natural arm extension, to hit slice approach shots, and to hit a better backhand volley than you would with two hands. And practice your footwork; a big, quick player is a lot more intimidating than a big, slow player, no matter how hard you hit the ball.

The Fail-Safe Eastern Forehand Grip

The Eastern forehand grip is a very solid support system for the racquet. You are going to meet the ball squarely right from the start. For the most part, you are going to have your hand behind the racquet handle as opposed to underneath or on top. It is a good basic grip to learn even if you want to switch to something else later. And unless you are purposely trying to hit with underspin, you will impart a little topspin to the ball, whether you like it or not, even if you think you're hitting it flat. Jimmy Connors and Chris Evert used the Eastern forehand grip and their records are not too bad. Pete Sampras's forehand grip looks like an Eastern, too.

The Continental grip, with the hand on top of the racquet handle, requires a strong forearm. It is a very wristy grip requiring a lot of feel. Many of the really talented players in tennis history have used this grip: Henri Cochet, Fred Perry, Rod Laver, Ilie Nastase, Martina Navratilova, and Stefan Edberg. Sometimes Edberg rolls his wrist over too early and the ball gets tangled up in his strings, causing a mis-hit, which he would do a lot less often if he used an Eastern.

The Semi-Western Forehand Grip

With the advent of such champions as Bjorn Borg, Jimmy Connors, and Chris Evert in the 1970s, the two-handed backhand grip was accepted as orthodox. Since then, the semi-Western forehand grip has been added to the list. Current stars who use it include Jim Courier, Andre Agassi, and Michael Chang. In fact, it has gained so much popularity and credibility that teachers are starting out beginners with it instead of the tried and true Eastern.

If you think of the Eastern as the grip with your palm aligned right behind the handle while holding the racquet parallel to the ground (as if you were going to hit the ball with your open palm), then the semi-Western is about halfway farther around toward the bottom of the handle. That position naturally closes the face of the racquet as you take it back and as you start to swing forward. When you combine the closed face with a low-to-high swing into the point of contact, you can hit hard topspin forehands almost automatically. That is why kids love this grip; they can whale away at forehands from the baseline, or whip sharply up the back of the ball for acutely angled spin shots that open up the court. The semi-Western also forces you to rotate your arm over on the follow-through.

There are a couple of big drawbacks, though, to this grip. First, it is not a versatile grip. You can't return low balls easily with it, you can't hit slice shots with it, and you can't volley well with it. Second, it forces you to make a big grip change from forehand to backhand. You may have time to do that constantly on clay, but you can get in trouble on faster surfaces. You may have trouble handling balls that rush you or get behind you.

The First Move

When you are playing at the baseline, you should wait with the racquet parallel to the court straight out in front of you. At the net, cock the racquet head up a little. Always cradle the throat with your other hand.

Your racquet head should be the first thing that moves as you prepare to hit a shot. A big difference between pros and club players is that the latter do not get the racquet head back early enough. The racquet head should move first and your shoulders should follow.

In the lower body, you should start to pivot on the foot nearer the ball as soon as the racquet head is right over it, and you should keep pivoting until that foot is about parallel to the net.

Unless the ball is within comfortable range and you can step straight forward into the shot, the next move should be a crossover running step with the leg that is farther from the ball. If you step first with the nearer leg, you have no momentum in the direction you want to go. The farther away the ball is, the longer that first step should be. Reduce the length of your strides only as you close in on the ball and set up to hit it. By then, your racquet should be all the way back.

Drag the Racquet Head

Your racquet head should trail your forearm into the impact zone on the forehand. Dragging the racquet head behind your arm generates maximum racquet head speed, the same way the last skater on a "whip" formed by other skaters moves faster than those at the center. Only at the point of contact should the racquet head and wrist come into alignment. It is the final link in a chain of momentum that began with your forward weight transfer and your body turn.

Topspin

If you watch such players as Jim Courier, Gabriela Sabatini, Michael Chang, and Andre Agassi on television, you cannot help conjuring up images of them whipping the racquet over the ball with a flick of the wrist for heavy topspin. The racquet face appears to get on top of the ball. But by the time you see the racquet turned over, the ball has left the strings.

The most common trap of club players who copy the pros is using too much wrist in an attempt to get topspin. Many pros *do* use a lot of wrist, but they have the strength, timing, and talent that allow them to succeed. They also have solid fundamentals that precede the adding of extra juice with the wrist. You should focus only on those fundamentals.

Once you get into a proper hitting position, you should concentrate on using your entire arm to generate topspin. Your racquet head should be below your waist and, ideally, below the level of your wrist at the end of your backswing. That will enable you to make the proper low-to-high swing into contact. The fulcrum of your forward swing should be your shoulder. You need the leverage of your large muscles, especially on the backhand, where your grip is weaker. The racquet strings should meet the ball just below the ball's equator, then brush up the back of the ball to impart forward rotation. Finish with your racquet head high. It is all right then to let your arm roll across your body naturally on the forehand, as the pros do, but don't flick it across.

There is no question that topspin helps tremendously because, if nothing else, it gives you a greater margin for error. But if you go out and just flick your wrist like you think the pros do, you will make more errors, not fewer errors.

One-Handed Backhands

To find a one-handed backhand grip, turn your hand from the Eastern forehand position behind the handle to just beyond the Continental forehand position on top of the handle (if you are right-handed, you rotate the hand counterclockwise). Once you get there, be sure to spread your fingers apart rather than bunch them up as if gripping a hammer. A hammer grip will force the racquet head to move ahead of the wrist on the forward swing. The shoulder, not the wrist, should be the critical lever on the backhand. Spreading your fingers will give you much better leverage on the shot.

A lot of beginners see changing between the forehand and the backhand grip as a formidable obstacle. They are so nervous and mechanical about it, you see them looking down at the handle to check if they have the right grip. I tell them, "Look, just like anything else, it'll come to you after a while. Don't worry about it, because with experience you'll learn how to do it without even thinking." Give yourself three or four weeks and you won't be looking down anymore.

Two-Handed Backhands

The principal reason people use two-handed backhands is that the backhand is naturally a weaker stroke, with a weaker grip, than the forehand. This leads to an initial reluctance to even use the stroke. If you handed a racquet to someone who had never played tennis before and all you said was, "I'm going to throw the ball to you and I want you to hit it," without mentioning forehand or backhand or giving him any other instructions, he would maneuver his body so he could hit a forehand. I have tried that several times and I have yet to see somebody try to hit it on the backhand. So to compensate for the backhand's second-class citizenship, you put your other hand on the racquet for more stability and strength.

The two-hander has some limitations and some advantages. One limitation is that you can't reach as far, so you are going to have to be a bit more nimble to get to the ball on your backhand side. Another drawback is that, in general at least, it is harder to hit with underspin. And that can affect your transition game from the backcourt to the net. Since you don't have that underspin or slice facility, your approach shots tend to be all-or-nothing bullets and you tend to make more mistakes. Few two-handers can change the pace effectively; most tend to nail the ball. And that is what you hear from a lot of critics of American junior players, especially the girls. All they do is bang away. Finally, two-handed backhand players' volleys are usually the weakest part of their game.

On the positive side, in addition to giving you more strength, stability, and power, a two-handed shot allows you to disguise your intentions a little better. You also can open up the court a little better because you have more control. You can definitely hit sharper angle shots with two hands than you can with one.

The Bread-and-Butter Slice

I would teach the slice as a player's bread-and-butter backhand. The slice gives you a range of conveniences you can't find with any other stroke. It is very energy efficient. You can meet the ball farther back in the impact zone and still hit a good shot. The high-to-low stroking motion naturally helps the ball rise over the net. Also, many other strokes come out of the same high-to-low swing path. There is the backhand volley, a very abbreviated form of the same slice, with a short backswing and short follow-through; the approach shot, with a shorter backswing and long follow-through; and the drop shot, with a long backswing and an abrupt finish. You can hit a teaser lob, too.

The slice backhand also gives you a high-percentage option on the return of serve. I think of the Rod Laver–Ken Rosewall 1972 World Championship Tennis (WCT) final. To this day, I do not understand why Laver served to Rosewall's backhand on the last two points he served in the decisive fifth-set tiebreaker. I would have lobbed it to Rosewall's forehand before I served it to his deadly slice backhand. Rosewall had an unbelievable return of serve on the backhand side. He would play for weeks without missing that shot. As it was, he hit two clean winners, the first on match point for Laver, the second to reach his own match point, and then he won the last point when Laver failed to return his serve.

The major drawback of a slice is that you can't hit the ball as hard as you can hit a topspin or flat backhand, but you can still hit it pretty hard. I think that's a small price to pay, however, for being steady and consistent with the backhand.

Point Your Shoulder

A lot of players are afraid of the backhand because it is the weaker stroke. As a result, they want to get the stroke over with as soon as possible. So they rush the backhand swing and pull off the ball too quickly by rotating the lead shoulder from perpendicular to the net to parallel to it before the ball has left the strings. To avoid that tendency, point your lead shoulder at your target all the way through contact.

The Service Toss

A lot of players do not realize, when they step up to the baseline to serve, how far in front and to the side they should toss the ball. Your body position is quite different after you've pivoted and come around to hit the serve than it is when you stand there sideways at the start of your delivery, with both feet and shoulders aligned perpendicular to the net. Whenever I demonstrate a service motion, I show that if you make the correct toss but don't move either foot, you cannot reach it with your racquet.

The ideal location at impact for the toss is about one o'clock, if you think of your head as the center of a clock face. But as you stand behind the baseline, you often envision one o'clock without taking into consideration that you're going to move. You'll toss the ball up front and right and it will look terrific; but when you actually pivot, swing the racquet around, and move forward into impact, suddenly the ball is not where you thought it was going to be. What was one o'clock is now twelve o'clock. My perception is that ninety-five percent of right-handed club players toss the ball too far to the left and therefore don't get their full weight into the shot. Many players compound the problem even more by tossing the ball straight up or back over their heads instead of slightly in front of the baseline.

You want the ball toss to be in roughly the same place on first and second serves. Just brush up on the ball more on the second serve to get it over the net with a lot of room to spare. For the average club player, learning to toss the ball in different places for first and second serves is just nutty.

Service Timing

When I was developing my game, I tried to pattern my serve after Pancho Gonzalez's. He was my idol, and he was known as the best server in the world, so he was a perfect model. Gonzalez had a beautiful, fluid motion. He didn't have a big, sweeping swing, but he had a perfectly timed rotation of his shoulders, upper body, and hips. Good timing and rotation are the keys to a powerful serve. The goal is to make the strings meet the ball just as the racquet head reaches maximum speed.

To get all the mechanical elements to come together at that optimum moment, slow down your swing at the start. That's what big servers such as Pete Sampras, Michael Stich, and Richard Krajicek do. Begin with a slow, rhythmic backswing, letting the racquet accelerate naturally as you swing it down, around, and up to meet the ball. None of those players seems to swing really hard or to muscle the serve, but the results are explosive—all three regularly clock more than 120 miles per hour on the tour's radar gun.

Use the Serving Advantage

Your serve does not have to be the biggest weapon in your arsenal to work effectively. Jimmy Connors never hit a lot of aces, but he used his serve intelligently to set up the rest of the point. He would hit a wide serve from his position near the center mark. So, from the first shot, he had his opponent out of the court, while he was in the middle. Right away, he would be in control of the rally. The only way his opponent could get off the string was by hitting a great service return.

A weak serve also can induce a return error. The receiver, knowing he's not going to be overpowered by the serve, thinks he can really tee off on the ball. What often happens next is that he hits it out or into the net. So don't sell your serving advantage short just because you cannot blast the ball at 100 miles per hour.

The Volley

If you are not shown how to hit a proper volley, you probably will take a full swing at the ball and not get very good results. The key to making a proper volley is to keep the racquet face open from the start to the finish of the short, punchlike stroke. Also, the racquet head should be higher than and even with or slightly behind your wrist. Look at pictures of the pros volleying. The racquet face is invariably higher and even with or slightly behind the player's wrist. Finally, the swing path of the volley should not be across your body. It should be forward, forward and down, to hit with a little underspin. Obviously, if the racquet head isn't up, it's difficult to move the racquet head down. All volleys, no matter how high or low the ball is, should be hit with underspin.

Try these two ideas to hit crisper volleys: 1. Synchronize your breathing with your hitting. Inhale as you prepare your racquet, then exhale audibly at contact. 2. Squeeze the racquet handle tightly just before contact and keep it tight until the ball is gone. That prevents the force of your opponent's shot from pushing the racquet head off line and helps you transfer the speed of his shot into your own.

The Half Volley

What you feel like doing when faced with hitting a half volley—tennis's short-hop shot played on the way to the net—is exactly the opposite of what you should do. The overwhelming urge is to come to a stop, stick the racquet down, and scoop or lift the ball over the net with an open racquet face. But the result will be a weak pop-up that either carries long or gives your opponent an easy sitter for a passing shot.

Instead, bend your knees, take a short backswing, firm up your grip, slightly hood the racquet face—I call it "covering the ball"—and keep your momentum moving forward as you follow through. Use the racquet as a wall, not as a scoop or shovel.

You are in trouble when you are forced to hit a half volley. Your only strategic objective is to hit the ball deep and continue moving forward to a good volleying position.

The Overhead

The overhead is a difficult shot because as the ball descends, it falls through the ideal contact zone rapidly. If your racquet is not ready to strike it at that instant and your body is not positioned properly, you will not make solid contact. Here is a short checklist of how to execute the overhead:

1. Turn sideways to the net.
2. Lift the racquet head up behind your head into the proper hitting position early.
3. Take small skipping steps backward, far enough so the ball won't come down behind you. It's a lot easier to step forward into the shot than have to reach back.
4. Get your body in a position that enables you to hit the

ball in the same ideal spot, in relation to your head, as on a serve. That means one o'clock (eleven o'clock for lefties) as you turn into the ball and face the net.

5. Keep your head up all the way through impact and into the follow-through.

The Lob

There is no question that the lob is the most underused shot in the game, especially among men. Why? The immediate answer that comes to mind is ego—the lob is not a power shot. People want to experience the thrill of winning with power. The racquets are built that way. Recreational players also don't see many top players, especially among the men, using the lob. Probably the best lobber on the circuit, man or woman, is Arantxa Sánchez Vicario.

Missed overheads, like double faults, often come in streaks because the shot requires precise timing. When your opponent misses a smash, he is liable to think about it too much. So if you throw up another lob, he may miss the next overhead, too.

Strokes vs. Shots

A shot is the combination of a stroke and the situation in which it is used. And in my mind, the most important shots are the second serve and the return of serve.

The Second Serve

The second serve is one of the most nerve-wracking shots. Even at the pro level, it is an important barometer of one's self-confidence. It's usually the first shot to show some vulnerability when you're getting nervous. So when people ask me how they can stop double-faulting, they are really asking, "How do I make my second serve better?" And my answer is, "Get your first serve in."

The shot that made me the most nervous was my second serve when I was playing doubles and I was down either 15–40 or 30–40. I also have noticed that double faults frequently come in twos. I recall when we were playing against Spain in a Davis Cup match in 1968 at the Clark Courts in Cleveland and Clark Graebner and Charlie Pasarell were down set point at 11–12 in the first. Charlie had just double-faulted, and now he was facing another second serve, from the north end of the stadium. He threw the ball up, it hit the tip of his racquet, and it went over the west stands. He and Graebner won in four, though, and we won the Davis Cup later that year for the first time since 1963.

The Return of Serve

More errors are made on return of serve than on any other shot. Receivers try to do too much with a return or they are intimidated by it. So, just as you should think about getting a high percentage of first serves in to avoid having to play

Russian roulette with your second serve, you ought to be thinking the exact same thing on the return, getting a high percentage in. If you were to increase your return percentage by just twenty-five percent, you would win a lot more matches.

There really is an art to returning serve. Some players are damn good at it. Jimmy Connors for most of his career got it back hard and deep consistently. Boris Becker's approach to the return is not to play safe or give a damn about consistency; he wants to put two or three blazers together and get the guy down 30 or 40. Stefan Edberg will use it as a vehicle to get to the net.

The First Volley

A quick way to become a more consistent net player is to hit your first volley crosscourt and deep, going for placement instead of a risky putaway. It makes your opponent move, allows you to hit over the lowest part of the net, and opens up the court for your second volley.

Chances are you will be hitting your first volley from around the service line. Then, step forward and veer to the same side that you hit the ball. Step in again as you hit the second volley. That means you will end up two strides closer to the net than you were when you hit your first volley, which should give you a good angle to put away the second volley into the open court.

Hitting on the Rise

A player who has the ability to hit on the rise and do whatever he wants with the ball has a rare talent indeed. Henri Cochet, Fred Perry, Jimmy Connors, and Andre Agassi, to name four Wimbledon winners, have been masters of hitting on the rise.

Hitting on the rise refers to the ability to hit the ball just as it has left the ground and is coming toward you, before it reaches the apex of its bounce. Few players can do that well because the ball usually is moving a lot quicker and has more spin on it than it would if you waited longer. But if you can hit on the rise, you can stand in closer and, as with the two-handed backhand, open up the court more with sharper angle shots. Because you're standing in closer, you can keep your opponent off balance or guessing a lot more. Usually your opponent gets into a rhythm of waiting to see what you are going to do, but if you preempt this process by hitting the ball on the rise, he's got no breathing space. Another advantage is that you're able to use your opponent's speed on your own shot. And you may have to run less if you play up on the baseline.

To hit on the rise, you must use a shorter backswing and a tighter grip. You must also hood the racquet face as on half volleys. Otherwise, the ball is going to shoot up off your strings out of control. And follow through. Remember, hitting on the rise is an offensive play, not a defensive one like the half volley.

The Offensive Lob

The offensive lob reminds me of the draw play in football, where the offense fakes a pass, drawing the defensive line in on a pass rush in poor position to defend a run, thus allowing a running back to scamper through an opening. There are two types of offensive lobs: the topspin and the teaser. A lot of your success will depend on how well you disguise your intentions. To hit a topspin lob, use the same preparation as you normally do for a topspin ground stroke, then pull upward abruptly at contact to brush the back of the ball hard, and follow through high, with less forward motion than on a ground stroke.

The underspin offensive lob—the shot I call the teaser—can be as effective as a topspin lob, but easier to control. It is a normal slice backhand stroke with a quick, upward acceleration of the racquet head at contact and on the follow-through. The ball should be just high enough over your opponent's backhand side so that he has to stretch completely to make his return. The underspin will make the ball drop straight down when it reaches the top of its arc. That usually will cause your opponent to hit his return downward into the net or to hit it very short.

The more successfully you use the offensive lob early in a match, the more it will help you later, because your opponent will back off the net a little, which will open up the lanes more for your passing shots.

Dink 'Em

Touch is important, and not just as an antidote for power. It really helps to have a little finesse in your game. It keeps you from being too predictable. A tennis player with touch is comparable to a baseball pitcher who can mix in some sliders and change-ups with his fastball. He keeps his opponent from getting grooved on his shots. Also, in many cases, a touch shot is a high-percentage response to something your opponent has done. If you don't have a touch shot, in some instances you will have to go with a low-percentage response.

We played a game called dink 'em, in which you couldn't hit it hard, but instead had to hit it softly with underspin into the service courts. There are all sorts of variations on that game you can come up with that will enhance your confidence in touch shots.

Unforced Errors

One of the key statistics you see whenever you watch a match on television is the category of unforced errors. Most tournaments employ statisticians to track matches for the press, most television crews include a statistician, and umpires keep track of some shots on their scorecards. However, unlike in baseball, the role of official scorer isn't regulated on the tennis tour. Consequently, there is no standardized definition of the term "unforced error." It is open to the discretion of whoever is charting the match.

Here is my definition: An unforced error is an error you make when there is no untoward pressure on you and you really should not make a mistake in that situation. You have enough time and enough space to hit the ball in the court. A forced error, conversely, is an error you make when you are in a defensive position or posture, when your opponent has the upper hand during the point.

Most often, questions arise about whether an error is forced or unforced on the return of serve. There, unforced errors, taken by themselves, may not necessarily lead to any ironclad conclusions. For instance, if you look at Boris Becker's return percentage at Wimbledon, you might ask how he has won three times. But he goes for a lot more on his returns than lower-ranked players who have lower unforced error percentages than he.

Your Big Shot

A big shot is not necessarily a powerful, spectacular one. It's a shot that never lets you down, that you win points with and extricate yourself from trouble with. Ken Rosewall's slice backhand was not spectacular, but it fit my definition of a big shot perfectly; it was the anchor of his game and he almost never missed it.

Pete Sampras's serve is a big shot. Jim Courier's forehand is a big shot. Stefan Edberg's backhand volley is a big shot.

Sampras deliberately goes for aces. Courier stands toward his backhand corner in rallies to make his opponents hit to his forehand. Edberg serves and volleys, and also goes to net behind some service returns, to get in position to use his big shot. Work on your big shot in practice to keep it big, so that it will be a shot that your opponent fears. Then, when you play a match, make your opponent hit to that shot.

STRATEGY

My Five-Shots-a-Point Rule

For club players, I have a comfortable rule of thumb. If, on every point you play, you hit the ball in five times, you are not going to lose any matches. Whether you are serving or receiving, if you hit your first five shots of the point in anywhere, even down the middle, you will win the match. Such a style may not be very emotionally satisfying, because the subliminal message common today is that the way to play winning tennis is to overpower the opposition, not outsteady him or outsmart him or outfinesse him. But steadiness is a habit; it is not something you turn on or off like a light bulb when you suddenly decide to play it safe on an important point. So start with steadiness; then add aggression and power.

Make Up Your Mind

Indecision is a common problem for many players, especially those with lots of natural talent who can hit any shot in the book. You can take too long to make up your mind and end up trying a foolish play. Try to avoid going through a lengthy selection process before hitting the ball. In most situations, there is a bread-and-butter play that works ninety percent of the time. You should rely on a spectacular play only ten percent of the time.

Most players tend to be indecisive on passing shots. They change their minds in mid-swing about where to hit the ball. There is no time in tennis for that. On passing shots, you can hit down the line or crosscourt or hit a lob. Select one of the three options before you get to the ball, and stay with your choice.

When You Get in Trouble

Aim for the center strap of the net. If the ball passes over it at a reasonable speed, it should stay in, regardless of where you are on the court. Moreover, the center strap is a much closer target reference than a spot on your opponent's baseline.

When You Win the Toss

If you win the toss, you can elect to serve or receive, or you can choose sides—or you can give the choice to your opponent. The only player who asked me to make the choice when he won the toss was the eccentric Dane, Torben Ulrich. He was deadly serious about it, but I don't recommend that you do it.

There are a number of factors to consider before you decide whether to serve or receive. For instance, would you rather be serving for the set at 5–4 or be trying to break to win the set? I believe it is much more difficult psychologically to serve to catch up. If you serve first and lose your serve at 4–4 or 5–5, you can always break back.

If I won the toss, though, I wouldn't automatically choose to serve. Against certain players, such as an opponent with a very weak serve or an opponent who was a slow, nervous starter, I would decide to receive, and then I'd go all out for a break in the first game. I was known as a player with a good serve, so I had that going for me in the second game. If I got the quick break, the important thing was to try to win a quick game in game two.

In my semifinal match against left-handed Tony Roche at Wimbledon in 1975, I wanted him to serve first because we were playing in the late afternoon and the sun would never be a factor for me on either side of the court. I picked the north end, so that when we started, Tony, from the south end of the court, would be looking right into the sun. If you pick sides, though, remember that your opponent then has the choice of whether to serve or receive.

The Important Points

The first point of the game is key. After that, the points on the ad side of the court are generally more important than the points on the deuce side because you are either building a two-point lead (going from 0–15 to 0–30, for instance), pulling even (going from 0–15 to 15–15, for instance), or winning or fending off game point (40–0, 0–40, 40–30, 30–40, ad in, ad out).

The Important Games

The first four games are important because that is the feeling-out period of a match, and no one wants to lose his serve. Once you go through a couple of sequences of holding serve, you are into the match and should have a fairly good indication of how things might go.

I think Bill Tilden was right about the seventh game, which he identified as crucial. As the set passes its halfway point, the seventh game is the place where you can forge or consolidate a winning lead, or, conversely, break your opponent's momentum.

Tiebreaks

Like the first four games of a match, the first four points are very important. One mini-break down doesn't seem bad, but if you get two mini-breaks down you've got a problem. Concentrate on consistency rather than on winning points outright. Get the ball in the court and let the other guy make mistakes. Later on, if you are feeling confident, be a little bolder.

The seventh point of a tiebreak is vital, just like the seventh game of a set. If you are ahead in points 6–0 or behind 0–6, it is set point. If you are behind 1–5 or 2–4, winning the next point gives you a glimmer of hope of pulling even (and can do the same thing for your opponent if you're ahead by those scores). If you are tied 3–3, you gain the upper hand if you win it.

The psychology of playing a tiebreak is different from the rest of the set. There is a lot more pressure on each point. You don't want to make any silly errors. So, above all, get the first serve in. In the tense situation of a tiebreak, you are more liable to double-fault if you miss the first serve. Get the return in, too. Make your opponent play.

The First Set

The first set is indeed key. Look at matches played in a Grand Slam tournament and ask, In how many of them did the person who won the first set win the match? Most of them. Winning the first set can set the tone for the entire match.

But, interestingly enough, there is one exception. If a first set is won or lost 6–0, sometimes it means nothing. I often was leery of winning the first set 6–0. Why? Because I had no place to go but down. There are lots of times when a player loses the first set 6–0 and comes back and wins. On paper it looks like it makes no sense, but it often happens.

Changeovers

You are entitled to take ninety seconds to rest when you change ends after every odd game. A lot of recreational players never even change sides unless they are playing in a tournament or league match, especially when they are playing indoors. But the changeover is part of the rules, and I advise you to use that valuable time, and to use it wisely. Never be in a hurry to get back on the court, even if your opponent is anxious to get the next game started.

Do more than simply attend to the prosaic details, such as toweling off your face, drying your racquet handle, and taking several sips of water. Turn your mind to the match and go over some of the things you were too preoccupied to think about during the heat of play. Even during the changeover after the first game, take the full ninety seconds. Reflect on the first few points. If you served, how good was your first-serve percentage? If you received, did you get your returns back in play? Try to keep your thoughts simple. If your returns are off, for example, you might tell yourself to aim a little higher over the net.

As the match progresses and you use the changeover to catch your breath, also use it to keep track of which shots of yours are giving your opponent trouble. Remind yourself to set up those shots more often. And be realistic about what isn't working. You may have gone into a match knowing your opponent has a weak shot, but now he or she is killing you with it. Be flexible and adjust your game plan.

When to Change Your Game Plan

At the very beginning of your tennis life, you are just learning to hit the ball squarely and get it over the net. The moment you start thinking about putting the ball where you want it to go is when you should start thinking about strategy. Strategy is an overall game plan to help you defeat your opponent under a certain set of conditions. In a best-of-three-set match, if you lose the first set you should think about changing strategy, especially if you lost that set by more than one break of serve. If you lost 6–1 or 6–2, you've got to regroup.

Usually sets that end 7–6 or 7–5, and a lot that end 6–4, went one way or the other because one player was mentally stronger than the other. It is rarely a case of strategy. It is just that somebody played the big points better.

The caveat here is that when you lose a close first set, you have to realize that you may be down psychologically. Nobody likes to lose 7–6 or 7–5. It means that you came oh-so-close to winning. The point I want to make is that you have to pick yourself up psychologically. That's even more important than strategy. You have to say to yourself, "Look, that set is finished. I played well. I almost won. Let's go get 'em."

You should always have a plan B, a strategic change. Before you go to plan B, take inventory. Ask yourself what has been working and what hasn't been working. You may decide that your game plan is OK but your execution has been lousy. On the other hand, you may be executing plan A flawlessly, not making any unforced errors, or not many, and getting your clock cleaned. If you haven't been missing much, then almost assuredly you should say, "My strategy's wrong."

Playing from Behind

I remember watching Rod Laver play Ken Rosewall in the final of the Pacific Southwest Championships in 1968. Rose-

wall took the first set 7–5—and didn't win another game. Laver just poured on the pressure with his bread-and-butter
shots—the topspin forehand and the slice backhand. Laver
knew when to strike to turn the match his way, and he did it
by becoming more aggressive with his best shots.

The key to playing from behind is to become cautiously,
not recklessly, aggressive. If you take too many risks, you will
go deeper into the hole. But if you concentrate on the finest
parts of your game, you will have the best chance of slowing
your opponent's momentum and shifting it your way. So
when you are behind by a set or down two breaks of serve,
take the offensive when the opportunity presents itself.

Make Your Opponent Hit the Shot He Hates

Every player has a shot that he or she would rather not hit. In
the 1975 Wimbledon final, I hit a lot of balls low and short to
Jimmy Connors's forehand. And in my role as captain of the
U.S. Davis Cup team, I zeroed in with my players on each
opponent's least favorite shot. If you can isolate an area of
vulnerability, preferably by scouting beforehand or by being
observant in the warm-up and first few games, you are a step
ahead.

If your opponent is shaky on overheads, lob a lot. If he
doesn't like to come to the net, feed him a lot of short balls.
Chip away at your opponent's confidence by making him hit
the shot he hates.

Percentage Tennis and the 1975 Wimbledon Final

Percentage tennis refers to a generalized approach to a strategy that will optimize your chances of winning the match. An example: When a group of my friends and I sat down at Wimbledon after my semifinal win over Tony Roche and Jimmy Connors's over Roscoe Tanner, we came to the conclusion that if I played the way I generally did on a grass court, I would probably lose. My usual game was a power game—to try to sort of bulldoze my way through the match, hitting the ball hard. It was a low-percentage strategy for me against Connors on grass.

I certainly had the stronger serve. I came to the net more often. Connors certainly had a better return, and he had better ground strokes. He had excellent penetration. So my strategy was based on adjusting my game: Make him generate his own pace on his shots. Go for big shots only when there is a clear opening. Since he penetrates and opens the court up so well, hit the ball short down the middle with underspin during rallies to give him much less angle. Lob over his two-handed backhand when he comes to the net. On my serve, pull him as wide as possible to get him off court to make a bigger target area to hit my volley into, which meant more slice and spin serves than flat ones. The day before, Tanner had served out of his mind and got eight games. Finally, avoid making careless errors.

The important lesson to be learned is that you have to build your strategy around what you can do. Don't try the impossible. The key to our plan for that Wimbledon final was that I was capable of executing it.

The odds the London bookies had set were seven to one against my winning. I think those odds would have been about right if I had played my usual way. But had the bookies known of my changed strategy, I think they would have cut the odds in half.

Another lesson from that final is that practicing with a hitting partner is extremely important just before a big match. The day before I was to play Connors, I arranged to hit with Australian left-hander Ray Ruffels before the final. After we hit some balls, I asked him to hit fifty big left-handed spin serves to me. He spun them as heavily as he could. So when I walked on the court to play Connors, I reacted to his left-handed spin serve automatically.

Give Percentage Tennis Time to Work

Percentage tennis can be evolutionary. You may start off deliberately with a plan that seems to be low-percentage, but you're doing it for a reason. Later, that same strategy becomes high-percentage. A case from my career came when I played Herb FitzGibbon in the final of a junior tournament at the Berkeley Tennis Club in New Jersey thirty-five years ago.

Herb was a net rusher. My coach, Dr. Robert Walter Johnson, said, "I want you to lob every time he comes to the net. Every time." We were playing on clay, so I could run down a lot of Herb's overheads. I lobbed every single time and he got tired. We were playing three out of five sets and I lobbed for two and a half sets. He got tired and I won 6–0 or 6–1 in the fifth.

Playing "Your Game"

I am reminded very strongly of an experience I had in 1966 when I was playing Davis Cup against the British West Indies in Kingston, Jamaica. The players were practicing right after the draw had been made on Thursday afternoon. Pancho Gonzalez was our coach. During a break, Gonzalez said to me, "How are you going to play Lance Lumsden tomorrow?" I said to him, "Well, I'm just going to play my game." And for the first and only time in our relationship as mentor–pupil, he reached over the net and he poked me in the chest and he said, "Wrong! Your game is whatever it takes to win on this surface today."

Meaning, if you lock yourself into a certain style, you'll tend to think of yourself as playing one style much better than another. And the last thing you want to get tagged with is, "Oh, he's a baseliner," or "He's just serve-and-volley." I'd rather be described as all-court. Even though I was, at that time, a serve-and-volleyer from California used to fast courts, I tried to think of myself as slightly different.

A great deal of the style you wind up playing, whether you like it or not, depends on the surface you play on most of the time. If you are going to play on a clay court a lot, you probably will not become the world's greatest serve-and-volley player. If you play on a fast court, chances are you are not going to wind up being a pusher. The surface tends to dictate your fundamental style of play and your strategy for winning. That's why the current USTA player development program requires our best junior players to play on all surfaces.

So while you may develop a style that would loosely fit into one of these categories, you don't want to limit yourself by thinking that you can be effective only one way. Your stratgic style of play should be adaptable. You should be able to change it to suit the changing conditions—the weather, the court, and your opponent.

Playing a Pusher

All beginners are pushers. You start off being a pusher because you are just trying to get the ball over the net and in the court. But as you improve, unless you decide you are enamored of the label and like driving opponents crazy because you can push better than anybody else, you will broaden your style of play.

A pusher does not like to go to the net. A pusher usually does not like to play fast. He wants to convey the attitude, "Hey, I've got all day, I've got nothing else to do. I'm having a good time. Let's stay out here four hours and I'll beat you 6–1, 6–1." A pusher relies on his opponent to miss first. So you want to draw him forward. You want to spend less time between points. And you want to be patient during the point, especially in the first game. That says to him, "I know you're a pusher but I can push, too." That's hard to do at the club level.

A lot of a pusher's success is due to the psychological edge he feels that he has over you when you walk onto the court. He figures you are going to wind up gnashing your teeth and breaking your racquet because you are going to be frustrated in about ten minutes.

I once played Harold Solomon in the French Open on the old Court A. A lot of people came over to watch Harold take me apart. I showed them. I tried to speed play up, taking less time between points without disrupting my own normal approach too much. I drop-shotted Harold and I lobbed him and I won the match in four sets.

Playing a Basher

A basher can hardly wait to play the next point, so slow down the pace of play. Get your first serve in so he can't tee off on the second ball. He wants to be in a position to hit the ball as hard as he can, so play the ball down the middle, short and low. It sounds suicidal, but it is a good idea because your opponent has to move forward and ease up on the power. Mix in floaters so that the basher doesn't get a consistent rhythm and has to generate his own pace. He is liable to make a mistake doing that.

Playing a Net-Rusher

Try some passing shots down the middle, forcing him to volley off his navel with little or no angle. Lob over his backhand
side. And get to the net before he does.

Playing an Opponent Who's "In the Zone"

When you sense that the other guy is zoning—i.e., riding an
incredible hot streak—it doesn't matter what your specific
strategy is. It is time to take a walk between points. You need
to disrupt his rhythm. Don't compound the zoning by making silly errors. Let him keep hitting winners. That sounds
self-defeating, but once he wakes up and realizes that he has
been winning all those points instead of you losing them, he
will start to miss a few and start to second-guess himself.
Then, as you keep getting the ball back and avoiding any
mistakes, he may go totally cold.

Eight Things to Do When Playing a Lefty

1. Close your eyes and imagine the path of the ball coming
toward you. On a left-hander's forehand, the ball is going to
come at you from your right to your left.

2. When you are returning serve, if he's hitting it to your
right-handed backhand, as most lefties do, take one more
step to your left before you receive, especially in the ad court.
Then take an extra step left as you hit, because the ball will
keep moving away from you as you swing.

3. If he throws in a kick serve to your forehand side in the deuce court, take one more step to the right.

4. On a big lefty slice serve to your backhand, especially in the ad court, the ball will naturally go to your extreme right when it hits the strings. So if you want to return it to his backhand, you've got to aim farther left. Take one more step to your left, but also take one step in, and squeeze the racquet handle tightly.

5. The most effective serve to hit on the deuce side is often a kicker right at the lefty. He will move quickly to his right and try to hit a cramped forehand from his left hip pocket.

6. If you can do it, also use the slice serve out wide to his backhand in the deuce court. But you know something? That shot is an example of how patterns create strengths and weaknesses in players. There are only a handful of right-handers who can really break off the slice far to the right in the deuce court. It is a neglected serve, because it is to your right-handed opponent's supposed strength. Pete Sampras is one of the rare players who can do it at will.

7. On the ad side, serve a slice down the middle T.

8. Avoid hitting a weak spin second serve to his forehand in the ad court. It's scary.

Playing on Hard Courts

The speed of hard courts can vary greatly from facility to facility depending on how much grit there is in the top layer of the surface. Some hard courts can be incredibly slick, making the ball bounce fast and low. Others can "grab the ball," resulting in higher, slower bounces, though not as slow as they would be on clay. The bounces should be consistent, though.

A medium-paced hard court allows both baseliners and serve-and-volleyers to play their games. Aggressive play, rather than defense, however, usually wins out. So even if you prefer to stay back, take advantage of short balls and go on the attack.

Playing on Clay Courts

There is a bigger premium on keeping the ball in play on slow, high-bouncing clay courts. It's true that your opponent can chase down more shots. Most clay-court points end on errors, not winners. You don't want to pass up a putaway or a sitter, but don't get overambitious. Also, pay attention to good footwork, because the surface is often slippery. Here are a few more rules of thumb:

1. Get your first serve in. Aces come few and far between, because the ball bites into the court when it bounces, slowing it down. Don't wear yourself out trying to blast the ball past your opponent.

2. Stand back on the return. You have extra time to get the serve back, so let the ball descend from its high bounce into your optimum hitting zone, and then make a slow, measured stroke. Once you back up, though, stay alert for angled serves into the corners.

3. Hit high balls back high. A lot of players think they

should hit down on a high-bouncing ball. Or, if they have a loop backswing, they sometimes have trouble getting the racquet head far enough under the ball to hit up on it. Take the racquet head back below the ball, then hit up, so your return is, in effect, a semi-lob.

4. Slide into your shots. It's the hardest adjustment for a hard-court player to make. As you are running sideways to the ball and see that you are about to reach it, stick your lead leg out, tense your muscles, and sort of glide like a skater into the shot. Try to time it so that by the time you have finished your swing you have stopped and are ready to recover.

5. Play it safe on low balls. You sometimes get caught reaching forward for a low, short shot because you've been playing deep behind the baseline. Step in and steer the ball back deep.

6. Go to net on very short shots, i.e., when your opponent's shot lands in front of the service line. Otherwise you'll be too vulnerable to the pass.

7. Vary the placement of your volleys. Once you close in, hit the first volley deep, then move forward and angle the second volley off sharply to one side, hit a drop volley, or hit another deep volley behind your opponent to the same spot as your first volley while he sprints to cover the open court. The slippery footing will make it harder for your opponent to change directions or run forward.

Playing Indoors

Conditions usually are about as perfect as they are going to get when you play indoors. You don't have to make adjustments for the sun or the wind. You don't have to worry about shadows creeping across the court. You do, however, often get an echo effect when you hit the ball; it isn't disconcerting, just different.

The first thing you should do is take an inventory of your surroundings. How high is the ceiling? How much space is there between courts and behind the baseline. Are the lights in the way on any shots? You can use the building's features as an aid to your strokes. A spot on a roof beam above the ball can become a reference target for a more consistent service toss, for instance. Be careful when lobbing; at most indoor courts, the peak of the building is over the net, but the apex of your lob is likely to be closer to your opponent's service line, which increases the chances that your lob will strike the ceiling and cause you to lose the point. Also exploit the side netting that divides your court from the next one. There is nothing wrong with slicing your serve wide so that it bounces into the netting, if you can do it. Just stay alert to the fact that your opponent may try to do it to you, too. So be a little more aggressive in your positioning on the return. Move in to cut off the wide slice before it curves into the side netting, and block the ball back with a short backswing and more of a punching stroke.

Whether indoor conditions are faster or slower than outdoors depends on the court surface and the facility. Surely a carpetlike court is going to be faster. Hard courts or rubberized surfaces may be either faster or slower. Indoor clay courts will usually be faster than outdoor clay; but they can also be moister than outdoor courts, so the balls will get dirtier. (By the way, I suggest using two cans of balls when playing indoors to maximize your actual playing time. Indoor time is expensive—why waste it picking up balls between points?) Conditions are often slower in courts enclosed in inflatable bubbles. The air being forced in to hold up the structure slows the ball down, so you can swing out a little more on your shots.

Finally, treat your body properly. When you come in from the cold, it is vital that you warm up thoroughly before you go onto the court. Spend at least five minutes in the locker room doing calisthenics and stretching exercises to get your blood moving. Ideally, you should walk onto the court sweating a little. Then, because you are playing in a heated enclosure in winter, make sure you drink water on changeovers to stay hydrated.

Covering the Court

Too many club-level players play as if they can cover the whole court, which cannot be done. Whoever configured the court back in the 1880s did a pretty good job, because even the fastest players today—and they are faster than they ever were—cannot cover the whole court very well. You have to try to get your opponent to hit the ball where you can cover it, and within that area you can be more aggressive. For instance, by keeping the ball deep to your opponent's backhand, you can expect him to play a safe crosscourt return. You then can edge closer to your backhand corner and set up to hit a big forehand. When you do that, however, you leave your forehand corner open, and if your opponent hits it there, he's made a very good shot and that's that.

Anticipation

Anticipation is tennis's counterpart to precognition in psychology. It is the ability to size up a situation and intuitively guess where the ball is going to be before it gets there. You start moving there earlier than someone who has to completely reason it out would move. It gives you a huge advantage.

Some athletes build their entire styles around anticipation. Lawrence Taylor used to ignore the defensive call and just follow his instincts; time and again he would make the correct decision. Magic Johnson, with ten players on a basketball court, would know where one of his teammates would be at a certain time and have the ball there when that player got there.

There is no question that experience helps you anticipate better. But experience won't help if you don't pay attention. If somebody hits a ball crosscourt to you, more than half the time you are going to hit it back crosscourt. The way a person holds a racquet has a lot to do with where he can hit the ball. When you're playing a person with a Continental forehand grip, you ought to know that he cannot go down the line very well unless he's on the run. And when he's at net, he is almost always going to volley crosscourt off the forehand.

I recall match point for Chris Evert against Martina Navratilova in the 1985 French Open final. Evert passed Navratilova down the line with a backhand. Navratilova should have covered the line. She should have been right there, using the percentages to anticipate. When you are playing anybody who uses a two-handed grip and you have pulled him out wide without enough time for him to get set and plant the back foot, ninety-five percent of the time he will go down the line or lob. Navratilova was looking for a crosscourt.

Snap

Steffi Graf has what I call snap. Snap is what athletes have when they are always on top of the ball. They have such a quick start that they appear to have uncanny anticipation. Michael Chang has snap too.

One sign of Graf's snap is the way she hits most shots with her weight moving forward, which often results in her leaving the ground at contact. She does that particularly well on service returns, when she seems to charge the ball. Also, Graf does not pose on her follow-through when she finishes swinging; her legs are immediately in gear and she is running for the next shot. She immediately transmits what she sees into foot and arm movement in the direction of the next ball.

Even though you probably do not have Graf's athletic gifts, you can work on developing snap. If you know from experience where an opponent is likely to hit a certain shot in a specific situation, you should force yourself to move that way as soon as possible. Try starting on the return of serve, by charging the ball intentionally as it comes toward you, as a baseball infielder would charge a ground ball. Your reaction time will improve gradually, and you will begin to develop snap on other shots, too.

Keys to Better Play

Here are eight suggestions on how you can improve your game almost immediately:

1. Play with a decisive attitude. Make up your mind where you want to hit the ball and hit it there, without worrying about your opponent. It is critical to do that on passing shots.

2. Mix up your shots. Be unpredictable to keep your opponent off balance.

3. Have a plan on break point. It can be as simple as trying to get the ball in play. Against a net-rusher, hit the ball crosscourt over the lower part of the net, giving you a better angle for putting the ball at his feet. Against a baseliner, return deep, preferably to his weaker ground stroke so he cannot hurt you with his big shot. If you return short, he may hit a winner.

4. Lob when you're in trouble. It is almost always a safer option than a passing shot when you are pulled out of court.

5. Hit approach shots down the line. A crosscourt approach gives your opponent too many open angles on his

passing shot. An exception is when you have a short ball with your strength, and the crosscourt approach is to his weakness. Martina Navratilova hit crosscourt approaches with her powerful left-handed forehand into a right-hander's backhand corner, and she didn't do too badly.

6. Cover the open angles at the net. That means moving in the direction of your preceding shot. If your approach shot or first volley is to your opponent's backhand corner, shade over toward that sideline because it is the obvious first option on his passing shot attempt.

7. Get moving after you hit the ball. You don't have time to stand there admiring your shot.

8. Practice with a purpose. Use a lot of balls, divide your practice time into segments during which you practice only one thing, and finish your session with a game to twenty-one points, switching serve every five points, or by playing two out of three tiebreakers.

TRADITIONS

A Little History

There are not many sports that have been played worldwide for as long as tennis has been. Of course, some version of running has been around for three thousand years. But tennis is one of those activities, separate and apart from being a sport, that have enabled people from various cultures and nationalities to get together on common ground and interact for centuries. So serious tennis fans should pay at least some attention to the sport's history.

The modern game is an adaptation of "real" (or "Royal") tennis, which became known as court tennis, an indoor game that probably originated in France in the thirteenth century as a form of handball called *jeu de paume* (from the French word for "palm" of the hand). In fact, the word *tennis* probably derives from the French word *tenez,* which means "take hold." Scholars think it was the call the server made prior to putting the ball in play in "real" tennis. The equivalent modern command would be "service" or "play."

Court tennis was known as the sport of kings long before horse racing was, because many French and English kings had tennis courts in their castles. There always was heavy gambling on the outcome of the matches. In 1415 Charles, Duke of Orléans, played tennis while imprisoned by the

English after the Battle of Agincourt. The Louvre, centuries before it became a museum, had two tennis courts. A tennis court was the scene of a dramatic meeting of the outlawed national assembly during the French Revolution. And King Henry VIII was an avid court tennis player. In fact, he was on the court at Hampton Court when he was informed that Anne Boleyn had been beheaded. One year on the middle Sunday of Wimbledon, I went to see that court with my HBO colleague Barry Tompkins.

In 1874, a retired English cavalry major named Walter Clopton Wingfield patented rules and equipment for an outdoor version of court tennis called lawn tennis. Later that year, tennis was introduced in the United States. In 1877, the first Wimbledon Championships were played. It was during that time, the last quarter of the nineteenth century, when most of the rules of the popular English lawn games—bowling, golf, croquet, cricket, and tennis—were codified to the point where they basically resembled the sports as we know them today.

More than anything else, history is that part of any endeavor by which you measure how effective the present is. It gives you a basis of comparison. When Hank Aaron was going after the home run record, the only reason people were so excited was that Babe Ruth had established the record.

Not to diminish the accomplishments of such pre-war champions as Bill Tilden, Fred Perry, Don Budge, and Helen Wills, but to me the modern era of tennis starts in 1946. World War II was a natural break; there was no competition at Wimbledon from 1940 through 1945. Starting in the 1950s, the sport became much more democratized, as the economy soared and more people started to play. The competition broadened considerably.

The most important year in tennis history was 1968. Wimbledon had announced late the previous year that it was going to let the pros in. Before that, the major events were for amateurs only; the pros had their own tour of mostly one-night stands. Wimbledon's announcement forced the hand of the International Tennis Federation. It voted in March for open tennis, and Pancho Gonzalez and Englishman Mark Cox played the first match between a pro and an amateur, in the second round of a tournament in Bournemouth, England, in April. Cox, the amateur, won the match. It took a little while, but the result was that all of the major events soon were open to professionals and all the old amateur players turned pro. That was the beginning of modern *professional* tennis.

The most unassailable record in tennis might be Rod Laver's achievement of twice winning the Grand Slam—a sweep of the Australian, French, Wimbledon, and U.S. titles in a single year—which he did in 1962 and 1969. To win a Grand Slam once is remarkable. But to do it twice? And even more remarkable, Laver might have done it more than twice, had he been allowed to play in those tournaments from 1963 through 1967, when he was a pro and the major events were open only to amateurs.

Scoring

I think tennis scoring is needlessly complicated. I don't know of many more games where the scoring is so illogical. You can just as easily say 0, 1, 2, 3, 4. But it certainly sounds more elegant to say love, 15, 30, 40, deuce or advantage, even if it sounds affected, too. The terms were Victorian holdovers from court tennis. There are several theories explaining their possible origins. The first is that they are based, imprecisely, on the quadrants of a sixty-minute clock face. Another is that they derive from the monetary system in France in the fourteenth century—when court tennis was booming—which was based on a standard unit divided into sixty smaller units (sexagesimal as opposed to decimal), with an intermediate unit equal to a quarter of the standard unit. The quarter coin had a value of fifteen and four of them made a full money unit, so games were divided into four points, each with a value of fifteen. The term "forty" may have been shorthand for "forty-five." A precursor of "deuce" is perhaps the French term *à deux de jeu,* meaning you need two points to win the game, and a precursor of "advantage" might be *avant,* one meaning of which is "ahead."

The original framers of the rules, I think, would have absolutely detested the tiebreak. Decorum was more important than the outcome to those in the English upper classes. And the gentlemanly thing, the sporting thing to do when the score was deadlocked at six games all was to have someone win two games in a row to win the set rather than break the tie straightaway. If you had won that 6–6 game, your opponent would have been given time to catch up, to prove he was good enough.

Certainly there is more finality to tennis with tiebreaks. There is nothing worse than renting a court for an hour and a half and having to stop with the score at one set and 3–4. When you look up and see you have only five minutes to go before you are finished, consider playing a tiebreak in the time that's left.

In pro tennis, most smaller tournaments play tiebreaks in all sets. But in all the Grand Slam events except the U.S. Open, and in the Davis Cup, the final set is still played out to a two-game-margin conclusion. While some observers complain that the rules should be uniform, I don't see anything wrong with the practice. It's good that individual countries or tennis associations can adapt the rules to their own traditions without destroying any important uniformity.

Protect Your Rights

You ought to study the rulebook so that you can protect your rights in disputes on the court. It sounds like an obvious thing to do, but many players don't know the rules. To cite just one common example, you win the point if your opponent puts the ball away but touches the net with his racquet as he follows through.

You should also carry a copy of *The Code,* a pamphlet issued by the U.S. Tennis Association that tells what to do in situations not specifically covered by the Rules of Tennis.

When you play without an umpire, the first thing you should do before the match is to come to an agreement with your opponent on how you are going to resolve unsure calls. If you are fairly sure of a call, make it. According to *The Code,* if you are unsure of your call, you must give the benefit of the doubt to your opponent. If everybody did that, it would be fine. Of course, some people may see things the way they want to see them as opposed to the way they really are. I like the guideline in *The Code* in theory, but it doesn't always work out in practice, since it leaves the match open to intimidation by the player with the stronger personality. So my advice is to agree beforehand that you will play a let when you have a dispute about a close call. Tennis is the most fun when it is played fairly.

The Most Abused Rule

Just about every amateur or club player abuses the foot fault rule. It is one of those things that separates the pros from the amateurs. The amateurs really don't give a damn, but for the pros it's a big deal.

Is it cheating? Let's put it this way. Cheating is breaking the rules on the sly. If you are breaking the rules and everybody knows it, you really are not cheating. You are giving yourself an advantage but you are not breaking any moral code. It is illegal but not immoral, I would say. It is exactly like a gimme on a six-inch putt in golf.

A Question of Ethics

The rules of tennis allow you to employ many interesting tactics. For example, I do not understand why more players don't use crazy serves. If you really practiced an underhand sidespin serve, you could drive some people nuts and win a whole lot of points. It is entirely legal, and I don't think of it as unethical.

When Michael Chang snuck up on Ivan Lendl to return serve on match point at the 1989 French Open, it was not unethical, it was smart. You are allowed to stand anyplace. You can go up to the net if you want.

Where it gets to be a tough call is if you move around during your opponent's service motion. You are allowed to move around a little bit. Zina Garrison wiggles and sticks her racquet out and dances on her toes. David Wheaton had Boris Becker complaining about his movement at Wimbledon a few years ago. Ilie Nastase used to move around all the time. And in doubles it is done a lot: the player at the net will move over to the center service line just before or during the serve. If you take a relatively stationary position and are moving in place or wiggling a little, that's fine. But if you are going from side to side with more than just a step, it might constitute interference.

Shaking Hands

Shaking hands is a vestige of the Victorian-era English background of the game. Shaking hands was considered the gentlemanly thing to do after intense competition. The tradition is a continuing reminder of the sport's upper-class roots. But I like the gesture. For me, it is a symbol of closure. It says you each have prepared and played as hard and as fairly as you could and the better player on that day won, but it has not been a life-or-death experience. What's done is done and it is time for both players to move ahead. A lot of the handshakes you see in pro tennis today are barely perfunctory. It is becoming an empty ritual, especially among some of the women. My feeling is that, if you are going to shake hands, do it right and look your opponent in the eye. That is what I was taught, and I still consider it proper and sporting.

Only once in my life have I not shaken hands with an opponent after a match. That was when I played against Ilie Nastase in the 1975 circuit-ending Masters tournament in Stockholm. I walked off the court leading 4–1 in the third set. Nastase's behavior had been so bad, and the umpire had been so unresponsive to it, I said to myself, "The hell with it, I'm not going to put up with this anymore. If he wants the match that badly he can have it." The officials retroactively decided to default Nastase, giving me the match. The next day, Nastase presented me with a bouquet of flowers and profusely apologized for his behavior. Ironically, he went on to win the round-robin tournament. Today we're good friends.

Tennis Whites

The standard tennis uniform can also be traced to the game's English origins. Those late-nineteenth-century English lawn games not only established behavior codes, they established dress codes. All whites were *de rigueur* in cricket, lawn bowling, and croquet, as well as tennis. Basically, I think, the decision was an aesthetic one: white simply looks good against the green grass.

Today, of course, Wimbledon still demands that players' clothing be predominantly white. And many old-line clubs in the U.S., such as the grass-court clubs along the Eastern seaboard, have all-white dress codes. In 1969, I was among a group that broke the color-clothing barrier in the U.S. Open at the West Side Tennis Club in Forest Hills, N.Y., by wearing pastel-colored shirts. But I think the predominantly white attire mandated by Wimbledon looks nice there.

Andre Agassi wears colorful tenniswear to go against the grain, to help jeans-wearers identify with him, and even to show his navel and midriff when he's pirouetting into a shot. A few years ago, when Philippe Chatrier, president of the French Tennis Federation at the time, reacted to Agassi's outfits by talking about imposing an all-white dress code at the French Open, it struck me as being a little late, closing the barn door after the horse had gone.

"Quiet, Please"

A lot of a pro player's sensitivity to crowd noise and movement depends on the importance of the point being played; he or she is more likely to complain if it is a key point. Some players use complaints about crowd noise and movement as part of their gamesmanship.

Sound, as well as movement behind the court, affects your ability to focus on the ball. Here is what I mean. When you are out driving and looking for an address you have never been to before, you not only slow down to read the street numbers but also, most likely, turn down the car radio. The sound of the radio is an extraneous set of stimuli that detracts from your ability to try to find the number you are looking for. It distracts you from focusing on what you are doing. That was the reason I decided to close my eyes for a minute or so on changeovers when I was playing Jimmy Connors in the 1975 Wimbledon final. I wasn't trying to rest and I wasn't trying to meditate, as some speculated. I was thinking about what I wanted to do. And if I had kept my eyes open I might have been distracted by both the sights and the sounds around me.

Having said all that, I consider it unrealistic for players, or ssshhing spectators, to demand total silence from the crowd during an exciting point. That is a ridiculous expectation. It is not natural. And the noise is only a distraction if you lose the point. You rarely see the winner of a point complain to the umpire about crowd noise. However, it is totally unacceptable behavior for a spectator to yell "Out!" during a rally. Leave the line calling to the linespersons.

The most recognizable tennis competition where noise is always a factor is Davis Cup. That is what separates it from all other tennis events. Players in Davis Cup absolutely have to get used to the noise and the partisan cheering that sometimes borders on hostility. It is going to bother you; the question is how you are going to deal with it. In order to get their players really to focus and concentrate better, coaches and Davis Cup captains have been known to have them play practice matches in the midst of a lot of noise and movement, just like a basketball coach getting his team ready to play in an archrival's gym.

My first Davis Cup match out of the U.S. was when we lost to Spain in Barcelona in 1965. The crowd went nuts. My worst experience, though, was in 1966 in Pôrto Alegre, Brazil. Our American ambassador actually warned us against cheering too loudly for our own team. The noise is most unsettling in doubles matches, not because you are trying to talk to your partner but because when a doubles pair is playing, the home crowd feels even more a part of the team. The home-team players feed off one another *and* the crowd. It was just brutal in Brazil with my partner, Dennis Ralston, against Tom Koch and Edison Mandarino. We won the battle in four sets, but Brazil won the war, three matches to two.

Different crowds have different cheering routines. In Germany and Scandinavia, they like to stomp their feet. At the Guayaquil Tennis Club stadium in Ecuador, there was always a group way up in the top of the stands under the Coca-

Cola sign that would ring a cowbell. The umpire would call for silence, but it didn't do any good. The fans would quiet down when they felt like it. The situation in which a foreigner receives the worst treatment in an individual singles tournament, unquestionably, is playing an Italian at Il Foro Italico in Rome. Even the texture of the noise is different. And you don't dare complain about a bad call. The Italian fans are infamous for throwing coins at the opponents of their heroes; they even did that to Bjorn Borg once when he was playing Adriano Panatta.

The Ultimate Experience

I was sixteen the first time I played on grass. I was competing in the 1959 Eastern Junior and Boys Championships at the West Side Tennis Club in Forest Hills, N.Y. Our tournament was being held on the club's clay courts. Word circulated that the touring-pro troupe, featuring such greats as Pancho Gonzalez and Lew Hoad, was coming through, and it was arranged for a bunch of us to hit briefly with Gonzalez. I got in line and got to hit about three balls with him. Later that year, I was invited to play in the U.S. Nationals at Forest Hills, where I lost to Rod Laver in straight sets in the first round.

Playing on grass is the ultimate tennis experience. The ball skids—quick and low. Hold your racquet tighter, get the head back sooner with a shorter backswing, and give it a shot. If you consider yourself a serious student of the game, you owe it to yourself to try it at least once.

The Newport Casino in Rhode Island, home of the International Tennis Hall of Fame, is the only completely public facility in the U.S. with grass courts—there are twelve. Anyone can make a reservation to play. Expect to pay upwards of $30 per person per hour of play. There was a wonderful ice cream shop right across the street called The Creamery that was a favorite hangout of all the players when we played at Newport. Several large resort-residential complexes now also include grass courts among their facilities.

The playability of a grass court depends on how hard the ground is underneath. The best grass court I ever played on was in Adelaide, Australia, at the courts at Memorial Drive. They were sensational. There were no bad bounces. They were level. They were just terrific. We won the Davis Cup Challenge Round there in 1968.

A Basic Play on Grass

You have absolutely nothing to lose by automatically hitting the ball to the open court on grass. The ball is going to be going fast and it is going to skid because the grass is slick. So you are going to force your opponent to run and stretch, regardless. Also, it gives you one less decision to have to make in the middle of a point when the action is so fast. Like the Green Bay Packers' sweep in the 1960s, which was predictable, if you execute this basic play well, it doesn't matter if the opponent knows it's coming.

The Most Exclusive Club

The All England Lawn Tennis and Croquet Club in Wimbledon, England, has fewer than four hundred members and a waiting list that goes on forever. That is why I like to say that one of the easier ways to get in may be to win the tournament, because Wimbledon champions become honorary members.

The All England Club has forty-one courts, thirty of which are grass and eleven clay (two of those are indoors). And yes, there really are croquet lawns in the back.

My 1991 membership directory included international tennis greats, such as Rod Laver and Chris Evert; British tennis heroes, such as Fred Perry and Virginia Wade; royals, such as Princess Diana (a member since 1985) and Queen Ingrid of Denmark; and a few celebrities, such as actor Charlton Heston. However, most of the members are British businessmen and -women with a strong interest in the sport. On average, they play at an experienced intermediate level of skill, although there are some strong younger players who compete for the All England's team in interclub matches.

The All England Club is not only the most exclusive facility of its kind but is also one of the great bargains. The club's share of proceeds from the tournament pays for the operation and upkeep of the club. Initiation fees and annual membership dues are each less than $100.

There is no question that Wimbledon is still the most prestigious tennis event in the world. My first trip to Wimbledon was in 1963. Having heard so much about it, I was most surprised at the understated austerity of the place. I had expected something along the lines of an exclusive U.S. country club. Even today, after millions of dollars in improvements, it remains a testament to the celebrated understatement of the English aristocracy. It does not have gold faucets. In fact, the amenities would not be exceptional at a mid-price U.S. club: the main locker-room area is still so small that lower-ranked players in the tournament draw are assigned to the "B" lockers under the Court 2 grandstand. That, however, is due to change in the coming years when another major expansion and renovation project is completed.

Getting tickets to Wimbledon is tough but not impossible. As a past champion, I get two Centre Court tickets every day and I get the right to buy two more Centre Court tickets and two Court 1 tickets every day. I always get the maximum.

The Toughest Tournament to Win

Wimbledon is probably the toughest of all tournaments. The reason is that grass is the surface least familiar to most players. If you look at the number of different players who have won Wimbledon, it is a smallish group compared with the number of winners of other majors. Wimbledon is a test of nerve and reflexes. There are very few lucky-winners at Wimbledon; usually the champion is one of the higher-seeded players. The pool of legitimate contenders each year is probably only four, five, or six players. One of them almost surely is going to win. It was no surprise to me that Boris Becker and Stefan Edberg played each other in the finals three years in a row, beginning in 1988. And, in fact, Becker, in 1985, is the only nonseeded male winner in history.

Competing at Wimbledon is an awe-inspiring experience. I used to be edgy even when I had to play out on one of the field courts. Winning Wimbledon in 1975 changed my life, elevating me from a tennis player to an international celebrity.

$28 a Day

I earned only $280 when I won the U.S. Open in 1968 while still an amateur. Runner-up Tom Okker got the $14,000 first-place money. Basil Reay, an Englishman, ran the International Tennis Federation. The ITF's per diem for amateurs was $28, the American dollar equivalent of £10 a day. The exchange rate at the time was $2.80 to the pound. It was ten days, so I received $280. It just shows you the influence of the English, who, even though they had no great players, had Wimbledon.

The ATA

The American Tennis Association is the oldest continuously operated national association among African Americans for any particular sport. It was established in 1916, and since 1917, except for the periods of World Wars I and II, has never missed holding its series of summer tournaments. Even though it is an African American group, its tournaments have always, from day one, been open to anyone. Several of its participants, such as Althea Gibson and Zina Garrison, have gone on to win USTA titles. I won the ATA men's singles three years in a row, in 1960, 1961, and 1962.

Trophies

I keep most of my tennis trophies at my stepmother's house in Gum Spring, Virginia, but I have four awards at my home in New York: my 1975 Wimbledon trophy, my 1968 U.S. Open plate, a small replica of the Davis Cup, and my Emmy award (which I won for the television adaptation of my history of African American athletes, *A Hard Road to Glory*).

You actually receive three trophies when you win Wimbledon. I got a miniature replica of the silver gilt Challenge Cup people see you holding up when they watch the awards presentation after the final on television. I got a miniature replica of the Renshaw Cup, named for Ernest and William Renshaw, brothers who won eight Wimbledon singles titles between them in the 1880s (champions after 1989 have not received this award). And I got a miniature of the President's Cup that was initiated in 1908 by Prince George, who later became King George V. The inscription on the Challenge Cup reads: "The All England Lawn Tennis Club Single Handed Championship of the World." That always confused me; I wasn't sure if it meant you were playing singles as opposed to doubles or you were using one hand as opposed to two hands. It means the former.

PLAYERS

Tennis Players as Athletes

Tennis singles is one of those sports that calls for a generalized set of athletic abilities, as opposed to say, football, where if you want to know how good an athlete someone has to be, you first have to ask what position he plays. If you play defensive line for the Miami Dolphins, strength is important. Speed and quickness, which are derivatives of muscle strength, are of lesser importance. And coordination, or fine-motor skills, helps but is far from the most important thing. But a tennis player must be well coordinated to hit the ball, fast and quick to cover the court, and strong enough to hit the ball hard and last five sets.

Since a tennis player must be a generalist, you probably won't find players who stick out in one area. For example, U.S. tennis players cannot compete with American sprinters or basketball players in foot speed, or with gymnasts in balance. David Wheaton, who has been in the U.S. top ten and stands six feet four inches, has a slow first step. NBA basketball players as tall as he is would run circles around him.

One of the reasons tennis in America lagged behind the sport in the rest of the world for a while was that it did not attract the best athletes by and large. There are a lot of athletes who, if they had played tennis with the same advantages as other promising players, could have been awesome tennis players, I believe. On that list I include Nancy Lieberman, Danny Ainge, Michael Jordan, Jackie Joyner-Kersee, and Cheryl Miller.

I also think we have not even begun to answer the question of how tall is too tall for a tennis player. Look back at the comments about Magic Johnson when he first was assigned the role of point guard. A lot of the old orthodox theorists said, "Hey, you've got to be kidding. He's too tall at six feet nine." Similarly, we don't know about height in tennis because tennis has not been able to attract the superior athletes of taller heights for us to find out.

Steffi Graf is one of the best athletes on the tour. Stefan Edberg is definitely a good athlete. Boris Becker looks clumsy but actually moves fairly well for someone with that much bulk. Michael Chang is a fine athlete.

Of course, athletic ability goes beyond measurable physical skills. "Intangibles" also factor heavily into the equation. There is spatial intelligence, the ability to figure out who is going to be where on the court when, and the skill to get the ball where your teammates are or your opponent isn't. Magic Johnson has it, and so does John McEnroe. Then there is determination. Is the player a fighter who will knock down walls to win? Pete Rose and Jimmy Connors come to mind. There is also the mental ability to figure out what is happening and readjust your strategy and tactics to turn a losing situation into a winning one. In team sports, coaches do that for their players. In tennis, coaching is not allowed during play, except in team events. Chang is a good example of a thinking player who recognizes when to switch to plan B before it's too late.

Sometimes the package belies the ability. Consider Chris Evert and basketball's Larry Bird. Both were great champions who beat generations of opponents, opponents who seemed to be clearly superior physical athletes but lacked Evert's and Bird's practiced execution, their mental toughness, and their intuitive understanding of what it took to win.

Men vs. Women

The truth is, Steffi Graf would beat *at least* ninety-five percent of all the men who play tennis. But against that top five percent she would have no chance, and she would not do very well against any halfway decent college player.

You are not talking about Graf and a male opponent having the same psychological pressures, though. Going into any man–woman confrontation, Graf would have nothing to lose. She would be able to go all out and see what happened. If she lost, the worst anyone could say would be, "I told you so." And if she won, it would be falsely interpreted as a female breakthrough, as in the Billie Jean King–Bobby Riggs Battle of the Sexes in 1973. The man, however, would be under intense pressure to win.

The competitive gap exists because men are just made differently. They are genetically stronger, faster, and quicker than women. Their muscles are more dense. And their upper-body strength, which enables them to serve and smash harder, is much greater. Yet that speed and strength gap is not nearly as wide as it was. Today, women are winning some races in swimming and in track and field with times that would have won a men's competition some years ago.

The man-versus-woman question came up again when Jimmy Connors and Martina Navratilova played in Las Vegas in the fall of 1992. Connors got only one serve per point and had to defend one doubles alley as well as the singles court. He won 7–5, 6–2. Both players received six-figure appearance fees, although the pay-per-view television deal was a bust.

For me, you defeat the very purpose for which you are having the event when you handicap the players. If you really want to see how a man would do against a woman, let the normal rules apply to both. By having Connors cover a doubles alley, the promoter was trying to handicap the match so that when it was over, either player theoretically had had a fifty percent chance of winning 7–6 in the third. Among other things, such handicapping supposedly encouraged betting action, and there were published reports that Connors wagered $100,000 on himself, which helped push him to become a 7–1 favorite.

But unequal rules destroy the appeal of such a match to me. And I also think if you want a true test, you have to make the man and woman play more than once and on more than one surface. They should play at least ten times, because anything could happen in one match.

African Americans in a White Sport

I get asked by kids about being one of the few African Americans in tennis when I visit schools during black history month or in some civics class. I think they ask because so many of the books they have read mention that I was the first black to do this, the first black to do that. The question is a natural one growing out of their curiosity.

The novelty of my situation wore off quickly, although it lasted much longer than I thought it would. In the 1950s, when Dr. Johnson started his tennis program, we all assumed that after Althea Gibson and then I made the breakthroughs, the same thing would happen to tennis that happened to baseball. It just didn't happen. A lot of it was because of the cost and the cultural barriers in tennis, as opposed to the abject racism that Jackie Robinson had encountered in major league baseball. Being in a minority certainly puts anything you do, right or wrong, in a spotlight, especially if you happen to be one of the best players. If MaliVai Washington were ranked in the top ten, whatever he did would be covered. He would receive more publicity than normal for someone in the top ten simply because he is black. It is because he is a bit of a novelty, and that is a news item. The same thing applies to Yannick Noah.

There are some advantages to being one of a small number of minorities in a sport such as tennis. But it is not so much because you are black, it is because you repesent an odd juxtaposition of things. People don't normally think of black athletes as being tennis players. It is an interesting opportunity if you are able to take positive advantage of the increased public awareness of yourself, to the extent that, as an oddity, you are much more widely known than somebody else who might be in the top ten. If you can combine that with an engaging personality, a sense of humor, and perceptible intelligence, you can go a long way.

The Top Ten

Before the advent of the computer ranking system in 1973, the only world rankings were unofficial, subjective top-ten lists compiled by tennis writers and tennis magazines at year's end. Today, the ATP Tour and the Women's Tennis Association issue rankings, weekly in the case of the men, and bi-weekly in the case of the women. The idea behind the computer was not so much to rank players on a week-by-week basis as it was to come up with an ordered, agreed-upon system for players to enter tournaments fairly, to do away with the favoritism that my generation and earlier ones saw in so many places.

The top ten is spoken of and thought of as something rather special. And it *is* special when compared with everything else. But numerically, it is even more accurate to talk of the specialness of maybe the top three or four. There is as big a difference between player No. 1 and player No. 6 or 7 as there is between No. 7 and No. 35—a huge difference. Tennis being a form sport, the same players wind up playing in the finals and winning much of the time. Look at the point totals printed in the tennis publications and you will see how big the difference is between their point totals and those of other players.

One of the most consistent criticisms of the computer rankings is that they are not done on a surface-by-surface basis. Players can earn a top-ten ranking by playing almost exclusively on clay. Then when they play on grass at Wimbledon, the most important tournament in the world, their seedings are based upon rankings that make no differentiation among surfaces. So you always have two or three guys who absolutely, in my estimation, should not be seeded as high as they are. I think that is a great disservice to the world's most prestigious event.

John McEnroe

McEnroe continues to fascinate fans, even in the twilight of his career. Andre Agassi also sparks curiosity. But there is more depth to McEnroe, more mystery surrounding his personality, as well as a much longer and more controversial track record in the public eye.

John is basically a very good and decent person. He turned down a $1 million guarantee to play in South Africa when apartheid was still legal there. I became quite confident of and much less worried about his basic instincts as I got to know him fairly well over the five years I was captain of the U.S. Davis Cup team. He was our star. I think deep down inside he is sort of shy. But he does not react to certain situations the way you would think someone of his background should react. He definitely can be rude at times, ill-mannered and surly, although not too often obscene. When someone is in his position, the object of so much press attention and in such high demand for such a long time, it is almost impossible not to be that way once in a while.

However, I have never bought the theory of some that part of John's on-court demeanor rose out of his being a perfectionist. A lot of people can use that as a crutch for their own inability to control their temper. John frequently would say, "I'm trying as hard as I can, so I shouldn't have to deal with linespersons who make bad calls." I don't think that, in the heat of competition, John realizes that people are people, that humans are fallible creatures. They make mistakes. Even John makes mistakes. I always say, "If you are really consistent and true to principles, then you will concede the point to your opponent when the linesperson makes a bad call in your favor, even if it is match point." Of course, with today's professional on-court officials, players are not allowed to call lines or the score, no more than a football player can unilaterally change a penalty call.

There is no question that John and I represented a clash of two differing approaches to playing tennis, maybe to the whole issue of sport. John always said, "I'm going to fight for what I think is right." While I agree that fighting for what is right is to be admired, sometimes he was plainly wrong, and he didn't know it. I guess, at bottom, what bothered me was that he wanted me to fight for him even when he was wrong. And that I refused to do.

Our most trying episode occurred in Cincinnati at the 1981 Davis Cup Final against Argentina. It was at the end of my first year as captain. And it just wasn't fun. John's behavior the first two days, and in the second-day doubles in particular, I felt, was poor. And Peter Fleming, his doubles partner, didn't help either on that occasion. They were playing against Jose-Luis Clerc and Guillermo Vilas, and at one stage it looked as if Clerc and McEnroe might come to blows. I forget what the problem was. But it got ugly. Afterward, John told a lot of friends and even me that he felt I didn't support him enough. I said, "I'm certainly not going to support you if I think you're wrong. You're asking me to bend my own moral code to suit your whims."

McEnroe's boorish behavior has entranced fans as much as it has appalled them. Why? One reason often mentioned to me is that he is a child of privilege, relatively speaking. His father's hard work as a Manhattan lawyer enabled John to grow up in relatively comfortable circumstances in a lovely neighborhood of New York City called Douglaston, in Queens. He went to private schools. His background is one of being well-bred, having all the advantages. So when somebody like that acts like the neighborhood bully, you wonder why. He is almost like a traitor to his upbringing. "Inexcusable," many have commented.

Another fascinating thing about watching John is that it was easy to draw the conclusion that his behavior got in the way of his genius. Here was someone who could do things with a racquet that no player before or since, in my estimation, could do. But you have to wonder, if he hadn't come up with all those histrionics, what he could have done at the height of his powers over a sustained period.

Everybody could plainly see his genius. But after a while, you came to expect some blowup at the wrong time. And the problem with the blowup is this: If you are a real tennis follower, it disrupts the continuity of your enjoyment. You are sitting there, really into watching a terrific struggle, and all of a sudden McEnroe explodes. It is like a five-minute commercial. Then when the match starts up again, you've got to get back into it. And if you are a casual viewer, you will go away remembering more of the histrionics than his play.

There is no question that his behavior cost John some matches, cost him a lot of support among fans, and cost him commercials. It even contributed to Louisiana-Pacific Corporation's withdrawal as sponsor of our Davis Cup team. On paper, John had the potential to be one of the biggest American athletes of all time, because he was so damn talented. He could have been a Michael Jordan of tennis. And he had a larger stage, because tennis was already big-time on an international scale, the way basketball is becoming today, when John was in his prime.

But more than anything else for a while, McEnroe's antics cost the sport. It cost the administration of the sport its reputation. The idea took hold that the people running the sport were cowards, that they were afraid to put him down for his obviously rude and sometimes obscene behavior.

McEnroe wasn't alone in this, though. Jimmy Connors cost tennis, too, for a time. There is no question, when you look at

Connors today, that he has been an overwhelming net plus to the sport. Following in the footsteps of such fiery players as Pancho Gonzalez and Ilie Nastase, he helped bring the game's behavioral norms out of the Victorian era and brought tennis out of the country club. But many times he took it too far. I have had sponsors tell me that they do not want to be associated with a sport to which they want to bring their eleven- or twelve-year-old daughter or son but feel they cannot because they don't want them to hear the sort of stuff that comes out of the mouths of the best players in America.

Throughout virtually all of his career, John has been outspoken, forthright, and, at times, as even he would admit, a bit too glib. I did not see him every time in post-match interviews, but many of those interviews became the talk of the press corps—hour-long sessions in which John seemed to unburden himself, which a lot of people thought were cathartic for him.

Finally, let me reiterate that, in terms of tennis talent, I have never seen anyone better than John.

Tennis Brats?

In general, tennis players are not that badly behaved today. The problem has been addressed down in the junior ranks for a few years now, and behavior has improved.

But there are factors that drive the trend in the other direction. One is that players realize very early that if they are controversial but good, it means money in their pockets. Controversy sells. Look at Charles Barkley. Look at Andre Agassi.

As I said, from what I've heard, John McEnroe and Jimmy Connors, on balance, went so far with their behavior that it cost them endorsements. They could have done even better commercially had they been better behaved. Both have been defaulted in tournament play because of bad behavior.

Another factor is that tennis players realize early on the power they have over their handlers, whether those handlers are their parents, their coach, their trainer, or, when they turn pro, their agent. If they are good, they get used to being catered to, even by tournament officials. So often they grow up not adhering to some group's behavioral norms. Instead, they do what they like. Human nature being what it is, if you are very good at what you do, you are going to be able to get away with more than if you're not. That special treatment for stars continues in the pros. If you are the big ticket seller or the marquee name, you are going to be given a little more rope.

The point penalty system that pro tennis (and most junior events) uses today has helped a lot. It enables officials to punish players on the spot as opposed to going through some legal due process, which was what the old system did. The old way took forever, and by the time administrators came to a decision, half the people had forgotten the incident. The biggest example of the effectiveness of the current system was McEnroe's default at the Australian Open in 1990. There is no question that it was a watershed event. And it seemed to me as if the world agreed with kicking him out.

Still, tennis continues to labor under a reputation of the inmates running the asylum, which began with the ascension of Connors and Nastase in the early 1970s. In a way, I think my generation failed to lay down some rules for those coming up behind us. We came up through a team-oriented development system. The generation behind me was epitomized by Connors, who came up by himself, with his mother as coach, and who answered to no one. He was a blue-collar kid whose attitude was, "I'll show those blue bloods." I believe that unlike McEnroe, who feels in his heart that his behavior is wrong, Connors thinks his is all right. He never apologizes. He just says, "Well, that's me." And he justifies it by saying the game was too straitlaced to begin with.

Connors *has* helped rid the game of much of the needless Victorian-era etiquette. But there is no question that tennis players are not penalized as consistently for rules infractions as, say, baseball players, possibly because if a baseball player is ejected the game continues. Not so in a tennis match.

A Few Thoughts on Some of Today's Champions

ANDRE AGASSI

Andre Agassi, the 1992 Wimbledon winner, is one of the most exciting baseline players on the tour because he doesn't just rely on steadiness. He is a shotmaker. While there are times when Agassi gets too creative in his shotmaking, often he is just being aggressive when he should. He goes for the big shot when he sees an opening. That is smart tennis.

The signature shot in Agassi's arsenal is his forehand. He tries to work a point so he can hit as many forehands as possible. And he likes to hit them while standing on or inside the baseline and taking the ball on the rise.

How does a player of Agassi's size—five feet ten inches, 150 pounds—hit the ball so hard? Part of it is talent; he has exceptional timing. But the other part is good technique, and it begins with good shoulder rotation. Agassi really turns his shoulders to take the racquet back as the ball approaches. As he uncoils into the ball, he generates tremendous racquet-head speed.

BORIS BECKER

When Boris Becker won the first of his three Wimbledon titles at age seventeen, I said that he was quite possibly the prototype of future champions. He is big and strong, at six feet two inches and 180 pounds, and he is also splendidly athletic and coordinated. His emergence signified, if not the end, then the decline of champions such as Bjorn Borg and John McEnroe, who had great talent but average size. While Andre Agassi and Michael Chang are exceptions to the trend, recent major championship winners Jim Courier, Pete Sampras, and Michael Stich all stand more than six feet tall.

Becker never showed any hesitancy or awkwardness, even at seventeen. He is naturally poised and confident. Indeed, he has always had a touch of arrogance about him, which all top players have to varying degrees. The thing I like best about Becker is his all-court game. Other prodigies who won their first majors as teenagers—such as Borg and Mats Wilander—achieved their early success strictly at the baseline. Becker has always been more versatile.

One reason Becker moves so well for such a big man is that he played a lot of soccer as a schoolboy, as did McEnroe. Almost any activity that helps you hone your athletic instincts will do your tennis game some good.

Becker has always reminded me a little of Jimmy Connors in his attitude. He relishes the combat. You can feel his enthusiasm when he's lunging and diving for volleys. At least until recently, he has looked forward to playing tennis matches. In tight situations, that attitude helps him raise his game a notch.

MICHAEL CHANG

The 1989 French Open winner, Michael Chang, at five feet eight inches and 135 pounds, is a tennis David facing six-foot-plus Goliaths almost every time he plays a match. He simply doesn't have the strength or leverage to serve as hard as Pete Sampras or hit forehands as hard as Jim Courier. So the foundation of his game is to get the ball back until he sees an opening to exploit.

While Chang often is at a physical disadvantage because of his size, he makes up for it with his mind. He is one of the smartest players I have ever seen. He goes on court with a game plan designed to use his strengths, such as his speed and lateral quickness, against his opponent's weaknesses. He competes hard. He always is alert to the ball and the psychological flow of the match. You can see his mind at work when you watch him.

The best opportunity Chang has to take charge of a point is when he is returning serve. He steps inside the baseline and uses his opponent's pace for his own shot. When he puts his return at the feet of a serve-and-volleyer, it forces his opponent to volley up. Chang is very accurate when he passes on the next ball, and he mixes in offensive lobs to keep his opponent off balance. If his opponent stays back and Chang hits a penetrating return, he isn't afraid to follow it to the net, where he is a sound volleyer.

JIM COURIER

When Jim Courier first joined the pro tour, people considered him only a clay-court player. He was one of the few U.S. boys to win the eighteen-year-olds' title at the Orange Bowl, which is played on clay, and he did very well on the South America clay-court satellite circuit when he started playing in men's events.

But Courier is not a single-surface specialist, as he has proved with an Australian Open title and a U.S. Open runner-up finish on hard courts to go along with his two French Open victories. He has worked hard to become a formidable player on any kind of court.

Courier has three great weapons: exceptionally fast feet, a lethal forehand, and a tenacious attitude. He has a quick, last-minute approach to hitting many of his powerful ground strokes. He gets to the ball with those fast feet, then uses a fast, wristy, compact swing to hit his semi-Western forehand and two-handed backhand. His short, swift backswing helps him disguise his shots, and his timing and strength enable him to really smack the ball. His favorite play is to shade to the left side of the court at the baseline and nail that forehand

inside out, to his right-handed opponent's backhand corner.
He will pound away in that pattern until he gets a short ball
that allows him to go for a winner.

Courier's I'll-bite-you-on-the-leg-and-never-let-go dog-
gedness reminds me of former top-ten pro Harold Solomon.
No one wants to walk onto the court to play an opponent
who never quits. But while Solomon launched moonballs,
Courier launches rockets.

STEFAN EDBERG

Stefan Edberg is the supreme serve-and-volleyer on the men's
tour. He's no slouch at the baseline either, although he isn't
going to stay there very long in any point. His backhand,
which may be the best one-hander in the men's game, is a
beautiful shot to watch. The only Grand Slam tournament
Edberg has never won is the French Open, but he reached
the final there in 1989, losing to Michael Chang in five sets.

Edberg gets a fast start to the net with his serve. He is at
least a yard inside the baseline by the time he completes his
motion. And because he gets in so far so fast, he can put the
ball away with just one volley more often than anybody else.
His volley stroke on both sides is compact and crisp, with no
excess motion of the racquet head. Less is more: the less racquet movement, the more effective the volley.

Once he is at the net, Edberg moves exceptionally well. He
steps forward as well as sideways when going to cut off a passing shot. That forward momentum transfers to his steady racquet head and gives his volley all the sting it needs. And the
closer he is to the net, the greater the angle he has to hit into.

Edberg almost never abandons his attack, even when he is behind. His opponent knows that Edberg is not going to let up. By continually moving forward, Edberg never lets his opponent relax.

STEFFI GRAF

I first saw Steffi Graf play at the 1984 Summer Olympics in Los Angeles, where she won the gold medal in the demonstration-sport tennis competition. Graf was only fifteen years old at the time, but I said then that she was the first can't-miss prospect since John McEnroe. She has since proved me right.

Graf's forehand and her speed are big weapons. She also has a champion's drive, discipline, and desire, ingredients that enable her to keep winning even though she has achieved so much already.

Graf has great timing on her forehand, which lets her generate terrific racquet-head speed for a lot of power. At times she looks like she hits her forehand late, and she sometimes does meet the ball farther back in the contact zone than the ideal. However, you cannot argue with her results. The key is that Graf gets to the ball early. If your feet are there in time, as Graf's always are, you can afford to be a little late with the swing. But if you are late getting to the ball, your racquet had better be ready to hit it.

Graf's snap, her alertness to the ball and quickness off the mark, come from her desire to play and compete. There is no point in being lackadaisical if you want to reach your full potential.

PETE SAMPRAS

Pete Sampras is a natural talent who can do almost anything with the ball. Unlike a lot of young players, Sampras is an all-court player who is more comfortable playing serve-and-volley than rallying from the baseline. He developed that style by taking a couple of big steps that are atypical of promising juniors but that eventually provided big rewards.

The first unusual step was to switch from a two-handed to a one-handed backhand when he was fifteen. With a one-handed backhand, he has better reach and variety. He can slice the ball with underspin as well as drive it flat or hit it with topspin. That makes it easier for him to hit approach shots and get to the net. And when he gets there, he does not have to change grips to hit a solid backhand volley.

The second step was to "play up" against older age groups almost all the way through the juniors. Some observers said that by doing so, Sampras missed the valuable competitive toughening that comes from winning when you are expected to. Another way of looking at it, though, is that Sampras was able to hone his serve-and-volley game without playing under a lot of pressure. Serve-and-volley tennis takes longer to master and you need more tools to play it than the baseline game. That is because the serve-and-volleyer is the protagonist, not the counterpuncher, in a match. A lot of young players get locked into a baseline style that allows them to win in the juniors but holds them back in adult competition. By competing against better players, Sampras could try new shots and strategies without worrying about winning and losing. He also sharpened his existing skills because of the higher level of play. It is safe to say that his long-term approach has served the 1990 U.S. Open champion well.

ARANTXA SÁNCHEZ VICARIO

Arantxa Sánchez Vicario surprised everybody in tennis, except perhaps herself, when she won the 1989 French Open. Since then, she has been one of the most consistent performers in women's tennis. Her engaging manner and tenacious fighting spirit make her a crowd favorite. Having other family members who play the game—her brothers Emilio and Javier are solid veterans on the men's tour—is a big advantage. They provide each other with support, practice, and advice. Making tennis a family activity can be fun, healthy recreation if you approach it with the positive perspective of the Sánchezes.

At five feet six inches, Sánchez Vicario has an ideal game for her stature. Her basic style is to get the ball back. She is very mobile and, except on passing shots, she usually hits the ball pretty high over the net, allowing herself time to recover and reach the next shot. The only time it makes sense for her to pound the ball during a rally is when she has a clear opening. She will also crack the ball with her two-handed backhand on the return of serve to put her opponent on the defensive at the start of the point.

The most striking shot in Sánchez Vicario's arsenal is the drop shot. It can be a dangerous play if you overuse it. But she defies convention: She drop-shots all the time, and she gets away with it because her technique is so sound. Moreover, she is not always trying for a winner. She makes her opponents scramble just to get the ball back, making them easy prey for her passing shots and lobs.

PSYCHOLOGY

What It Takes to Win

It is not just the more talented player who wins. Some players may try a little harder. Some players may be a little smarter with strategy and tactics. Some players may be in better shape. Some players may have a better temperament for the game. All of those things, added up, can negate a talent advantage. For instance, if you ask who was more talented in his prime, John McEnroe or Jimmy Connors, it's no contest: McEnroe. But if you look at the numbers of pro tournaments each has won, there is no comparison: Connors has one hundred and nine, McEnroe has seventy-seven. (Connors also leads in Grand Slam singles titles, eight to seven.) To be a winner, you must be a fierce competitor as well as a shotmaker.

Relish the Combat

No one loves the competition of a tennis match more than Jimmy Connors, especially when he's playing in front of a big crowd. He reminds me of a feisty welterweight boxer; he loves mixing it up. In Connors's code, you run for everything and spill your guts out to win a match. The sheer intensity of your competitive fire may be enough to overcome an opponent with more firepower in his strokes.

Connors is an extreme example of how you can get the psychological edge on your opponent by the body language you display on court. You should try to give the impression that you are always thinking, "Hey, I'm going to win this match." Connors's finger wagging and other gestures are aimed at telling his opponent that Connors has the upper hand. Against many opponents, that body language makes him an intimidating presence.

Regardless of how distressed or frustrated you feel, don't let your opponent know that he's got you rattled. Always try to look like a winner, even if you are behind. You shouldn't be obnoxious about it, because you might make your opponent want to beat you even more. But a sustained look of control and confidence can give you a mental edge that results in victory.

See Yourself Succeeding

I think it is very important as you progress to see yourself play and to match that image against what your instructor says is ideal. That's why you ought to choose a teaching pro who has video equipment. Don't be afraid to check yourself out. It is also useful to watch some instruction videos of experts with smooth strokes.

How does all this help? Pancho Gonzalez told me that whenever he thought a stroke of his was a little off, he would close his eyes and picture himself hitting the shot perfectly. You, too, should have in your mind the image of yourself hitting the ball perfectly. You can think about it when things are going wrong or when you get nervous. Close your eyes before the point begins, see yourself executing the shot, then open your eyes and do it, without worrying too much about the result.

Coping with Choking

Everybody chokes. I don't care who you are, Rod Laver, Billie Jean King, John McEnroe, Andre Agassi, or Steffi Graf, everybody chokes at one time or another. There are different ways that choking manifests itself, but the most common is hitting the ball so tentatively that it lands short or goes straight into the net. Some players, though, react in the opposite way, by hitting the ball so hard that it winds up in the fence.

One thing to do when you find yourself getting nervous during a tight situation, such as serving for the match, is to take your time. Many players rush when they are choking, because they want to get the pressure situation over with. Instead, follow your usual pre-point routine and take some big, measured breaths before each big point. If you can slow down physiologically, you can start to get a little more control of the situation.

Second, control your body language. If you are really disappointed because you just made a tentative error and you put your hand up to your head and look up into the sky in disgust, what you are doing is exaggerating a defeatist emotion inside you. When you are nervous, it is really the time to put your head down and focus your eyes on your racquet strings to regain your composure, let all your muscles relax, then straighten up and look confident and aggressive as you move into position for the next point. It isn't easy to go through what may seem like contrived actions to fight to keep your ship on an even keel, but it definitely helps. I even liked to get a little mad at the situation as a way of psyching myself up to produce my best. It was almost like I was saying to myself, "The people watching and my opponent all think I'm going to choke, but watch, I'll show them."

Third, reduce your decision making during the big point by planning the point before you step up to the baseline to begin your delivery. Decide where you are going to aim your serve, whether you are going to go to the net or stay back, and whether you are going to direct the rest of your shots toward your opponent's forehand or backhand.

Finally, just execute. Don't worry about the results. You want to say to yourself afterward, whether you made an error or not, "I played this point and hit the shot just the way I was supposed to." If you did that and still lost, you can live with yourself.

Handling the Elements

My teacher Dr. Johnson stressed the importance of a positive mental approach to dealing with such adverse conditions as bright sun or high winds. The worse the conditions are, the better for you—if you have the right outlook—because they are driving the other player nuts. Jim Loehr, the leading instructor in the mental aspects of the game today, tells his pupils to react to trying conditions by thinking, "I love it."

If you are playing under a bright sun, move your position along the baseline when you are serving to prevent being blinded. That's easier than adjusting the location of your toss. Wear a hat, and try wearing dark glasses. And don't hesitate to lob into the sun. If you are playing in a crosswind, aim farther inside the sidelines than you normally would. The harder you hit, the less the wind will affect your shots. When the wind is behind you, your shots will go faster and your opponent's will go slower, so you should be ready to attack short balls and try to get to the net. When the wind is against you, swing out on all your shots and aim a little higher over the net. In both sunny and windy conditions, be careful on overheads: unless the lob is a sitter, it is often prudent to let the ball bounce before you smash.

Sports Psychologists

A decade ago, sports psychology was still in its infancy. Since then, though, such champions as Gabriela Sabatini and Pat Cash have gone so far as to thank their sports psychologists in their post-victory comments at the U.S. Open and Wimbledon, respectively. Moreover, sports psychology has become another tool for rising pro and college players to use in an effort to close the gap with those ranked above them. And for promising juniors and their parents, sports psychology can be especially helpful when dealing with the pressures of that arena. The next frontier is at the level of skilled local players who either compete in tournaments or take their recreational games very seriously. They, too, now realize that perfecting specific mental skills for tennis can have as critical an impact as perfecting physical skills.

So sports psychology is very relevant to tennis players. On the court, the outcome of a close match often boils down to which player wins four or five key points. If you are losing such matches, it may be because the other guy is a little tougher mentally. You need to learn to control your emotions on the court so that you can play as well as you are able. That sounds simplistic, but it is true. If you can maintain a positive psychological approach to the challenges that tennis presents, you will start winning more of those points and more matches.

Sports psychology is increasingly important in a broader sense for elite players, especially juniors and up-and-coming young pros. The competition is incredibly stiff these days, and there is a perception that so much more is at stake now than in years past because of the huge amounts of money to be made in pro tennis and because so much has been spent on the development of these players. The pressures they feel are tremendous: pressures on their own sense of self-esteem; pressures from parents, coaches, officials, and agents; pressures from the demands of integrating tennis with the process of growing up and living a full, balanced life. A sports psychologist can help you deal with both the on-court and off-court elements of your tennis life.

WISDOM

Setting Up Your Playing Schedule

A lot of young pros play too much too early. They do it because they want to get their computer rankings up high as fast as possible. Then, to protect their rankings, they begin to play only in events where the conditions favor their game. If playing too much doesn't cause burnout, playing schedules that are too restrictive can hinder their development. For example, I think all young pros should play Wimbledon simply for the experience, if their rankings are high enough to merit entry. But some of them skip the game's biggest event because the grass courts are not suited to their game, and they would probably lose in an early round.

Whenever possible, you, too, should vary your playing schedule. It can be tough to do. But if your court time is usually limited to hard courts and you get an invitation to play on clay, do it. Also, seek out new opponents. The same old Saturday morning game can sap your interest in tennis if it's not fun.

How to Practice

Human nature being what it is, people love to play. But if you really want to get better, you have to practice. Ideally it should be a 2:1 ratio of play to practice. But a 3:1 ratio is pretty good. Have a plan in mind as to what you are practicing that day and for how long. Practice is helpful if you are correctly repeating what you should be doing. Correct repetition is the way to perfect your strokes.

Conditioning

Vic Braden, when asked, "What's the first thing I should do to improve my tennis?" always answered, "Lose five pounds." There is some truth to that.

Most people probably play at a level or pace commensurate with their conditioning. If you improved your conditioning, you could play a lot more and a lot better.

It is a bit of a chicken-and-egg situation. You can use tennis to get into shape, or you can get into shape and then make the best use of the time you have playing tennis. If you just use tennis to get yourself in shape as you are learning, there are limitations to what you will be able to do on the court. But if you make it a point to get into shape by working out off the court as you are learning to play, certainly the game is going to be a lot more enjoyable.

Get Your Motor Running

After my heel surgery in 1977, I developed a warm-up routine I would go through every time I played or practiced. I would run around the court two or three times, run in place for a minute or two, and then go through a series of stretches. I would begin the stretching with head rolls. Then I would shrug my shoulders, wave my arms both vertically and horizontally, bend to both sides from the waist, do a couple of deep knee bends, touch my toes, and then spread my legs and bend over to draw an imaginary circle on the court. I would finish by jumping straight up as high as I could ten times without stopping.

The entire routine took six or seven minutes. When I hit the first ball, it was amazing. I felt like I was already in third gear and ready to shift into fourth. I began the 1978 season ranked No. 257 on the computer and finished it at No. 13. And I turned thirty-five years old in July of that year.

I recommend you begin your precourt warm-up by pedaling for just five minutes on a stationary bike (which I think all clubs should have in their locker rooms) or by riding your bike to the courts, followed by a stretching routine like mine. You'll feel better and play better.

The "M" Drill

Here is a simple movement exercise to help you warm up before playing or to help you improve your mobility. Start at the right-hand corner of the court, where the baseline meets the doubles sideline. Sprint forward and touch the net, then shuffle sideways to the singles sideline. From there, backpedal to the service line, shuffle sideways to the center service line, then sprint forward to touch the net at the strap. Backpedal straight back to the service line, shuffle sideways to the other singles sideline, sprint forward and touch the net, shuffle sideways to that doubles sideline, backpedal all the way to the baseline, then turn and sprint to the corner where you started. If you draw the pattern out on a piece of paper, you'll see a big letter "M" that you've traced in the forecourt.

Tennis Elbow

If you play a lot, tennis elbow may be unavoidable. That is because it can come on strictly because of overuse of those muscles and tendons around the joint. The first thing to do to avoid it is make sure that you stroke the ball properly, which means that you ought to have your strokes reviewed periodically in a lesson with a teaching pro. A leading cause of tennis elbow is letting your elbow lead the swing when you hit your backhand.

I got tennis elbow in late 1968. It came upon me literally overnight, and I will never forget it. We were in Puerto Rico getting ready to play India in a Davis Cup match several weeks after I won the U.S. Open. One morning I went out to practice and when I started to warm up, all of a sudden my elbow was hurting. The day before, it did not hurt.

It was a problem I had for almost a year. I eventually got a cortisone injection from Dr. Theodore Fox, who was the Chicago Bears' team doctor. It definitely helped. But I also had to change my service motion. Eventually the tennis elbow went away. But it was not until the 1970 Australian Open, which I won in January of that year, that I really started to feel that I could go all out without hurting myself.

If you start feeling twinges in your elbow, immediately

start treating it with ice to reduce the inflammation, and massage it to get fresh blood flowing to the area to help it heal. Rest, too. I also would strongly suggest you go to your local sports medicine clinic, which are now as omnipresent as McDonald's. Tennis elbow is as common as a cold, so the experts there will have good advice about what to do.

Picking a Teaching Pro

When considering a teacher, the first thing to do is to look at his or her credentials, like the credentials for a doctor or a lawyer or any other professional. Many teaching pros are certified. The two groups that do certifying are the U.S. Professional Tennis Association (USPTA) and the U.S. Professional Tennis Registry (USPTR). The USPTA is the older organization and the more open-minded in its evaluation of the proper way to teach. I am a USPTA-certified pro. The USPTR endorses a more specific teaching methodology in its accreditation process. What both organizations do in certifying teachers is establish, by tests, that the instructors know, are able to demonstrate, and are able to teach the fundamentals of the sport.

The best teachers usually belong to both groups, though some very good ones belong to neither. I was taught initially by a college student, Ron Charity, who knew what he was doing. Later, the teacher I was most associated with was Dr. Robert Walter Johnson. Neither belonged to a professional tennis teachers organization at the time.

The second step in selecting a pro is to check references.

Ask players you know how good a pro is, and whether he is best with beginners or with advanced players, with groups or with a single student. Is he fun to be with or a no-nonsense drill sergeant? When picking a pro for your child, it is crucial that he be patient, understanding, innovative, and creative. In fact, teaching children is an art in itself. Just as Bill Parcells might be out of his element teaching Pop Warner Football, so too may the best-known tennis pro in your area be ill-equipped to teach your child. Also, if you are an advanced player looking for help with a specific stroke, ask if the teacher has areas of specialization. Some may be better teachers of ground strokes, others may be better on the serve.

I took my first volley lesson from Buzzy Hattleman, a pro in Baltimore. My serve was honed under the guidance of Pancho Gonzalez when I attended UCLA. And my UCLA coach, J. D. Morgan, was a strong influence in terms of strategy and psychology. The point is, even if you have a primary pro, it is silly not to seek out some other advice. It is likely that your pro can recommend another teacher who can help you with a specific stroke, just as your primary doctor might send you to a specialist.

Third, consider where a pro does his teaching. If a pro is based at a prestigious club, you can expect he really knows what he's doing and has a lot of experience. This is a tricky issue, though. There are a lot of very good teachers who have spent their entire careers at public parks. Two very good examples are Jimmy Evert, Chris's father, and John Wilkerson, the longtime coach of pros Zina Garrison and Lori McNeil. So another reference factor that may apply for you is whether

the teacher has coached any players who have gone on to elite
success.

Fourth, look for a pro who has state-of-the-art equipment.
Video capability today is a near necessity for anybody who
wants to be considered in the top echelon.

Fifth, investigate whether the pro whose name is on the
program actually spends hours on the court teaching or simply delegates lessons to his assistants and spends all his time
running the operation from his office. It's a little like when I
was trying to find a doctor to do my heart bypass operations.
I wanted to know how many times he had done the proce-
dure, not whether he taught it at medical school.

Sixth, don't necessarily assume that a onetime great player
makes an excellent teaching pro. Many of the best teachers
were, at best, also-rans in competitive tennis. There are some
situations, of course, where past tournament success certainly
is a valuable aid—not so much in the teaching of strokes but
in the strategy and psychology of a playing situation.

Write It Down

A notebook should be an integral part of your equipment.
When you are learning the game, keep notes on your lessons.
So many things pop up that if you record your learning process in diary form, you will be amazed at how much valuable
information you will gather. Then when you go out to practice, pull out your notebook and devise a specific plan of how
to use the time you have allotted.

Once you begin to play matches, use your notebook to

keep track of how you do in competition. At the end of a match, put your thoughts down in writing. First, record the basics of the match, such as the opponent and the score. Then write a brief rough summary of such critical factors as double faults, return of serve errors, and ad points lost. Don't worry about compiling a precise tally; the notes are merely to remind you of the areas of your game that need work. Use them as a guide to plan your next practice session.

Last, like baseball hitters and pitchers, write down specific observations about your opponent's game. At what pace does the opponent play—fast or slow? What are his serving tendencies at 15–30 and 30–40? Does he move better to his right or to his left, and how well does he move forward and backward? What shots does he never hit? Recreational players tend to play the same opponents quite often. You should be able to build up a good catalogue of your opponent's tendencies. If you know what he is going to do before you step onto the court, your chances of winning increase.

Get a Second Opinion

Tennis is an individual sport, but good coaching is a big help. Even if you are an accomplished player, you should let a reputable teaching pro take a look at your game every so often and have a friend chart a couple of your matches. As you start to move up the tournament ladder, seek advice from a better, more experienced player. The veteran not only can give you some hints on the subtleties of match play, but also may be a terrific source of information on other players and their games. Friends and family can make life easier by dealing with off-court details and distractions during a tournament, as well as by lending important moral support.

Computers

Computers are here to stay in tennis. Biomechanics analysts use them to break down muscle movements in a player's strokes. On the U.S. Davis Cup teams when I was captain, we used them to chart a player's shots. We had experts from the firm CompuTennis scout our upcoming opponents. Dick Gould, the longtime coach at Stanford, has taught all his varsity players how to chart matches with a computer. The result is that players know from hard statistics what their strengths and weaknesses are, as well as those of their opponents. They can develop more detailed, concrete game plans. A coach's suggestions are buttressed by solid data. If you know from a computer that an opponent makes more errors on the forehand volley, you won't hesitate to hit to it on a big point. Computers help take the indecisiveness out of your shot selection.

If your teaching pro doesn't have a computer yet, be patient. I believe a computer will eventually be a standard part of any good tennis instructor's equipment. With the computer, the pro will have a valuable second opinion about the areas of your game that need improvement, and he will have the statistics to back it up.

Why Play Doubles?

Doubles forces you to play the entire court, whether you like it or not. You do not have any choice, whereas in singles you can think of yourself as strictly a baseliner and stay back there. Doubles also is mentally stimulating. Your mind has to work quicker. You also learn to develop anticipation, which will be good for you in singles.

There are four shots that you can hone by playing a lot of doubles. One is the return of serve. You become accustomed to aiming at a small target area. The second is the spin serve. A cardinal rule of doubles is to get a high percentage of first serves in, and the way to do that is to use a second serve for your first delivery. The third is the volley. The first volley in doubles is pressure-packed, because if you miss too many, you will lose your serve and let your team down. And the fourth is the lob. It's the way for you and your partner to take the net away from your opponents. You are going to lob more in one doubles match than you might in a week of singles.

Choosing Receiving Sides in Doubles

I go around and around on the question of choosing which side to play on. There are several factors to consider.

You usually put the finesse player or steady player on the forehand side, somebody who, when the other team is serving, has the job of just getting the ball back in the court; nothing flashy, not trying to hit winners, but simply making the serving team play. The idea is that it is very risky to take chances on that first point, or when the score is tied at 15–15, 30–30, or deuce. If you give the serving team a free first point, the odds of the serving team holding serve increase substantially. The whole psychology of a game changes when the serving team is down 0–15. And if you get a 15–30 or 30–40 lead and a second serve, then the flashier player in the ad court might go for it on the return.

The person with the stronger forehand should play the backhand *provided his or her backhand return of serve is decent.* That puts his forehand and forehand volley in the middle, where most balls come in doubles. If the person with the better forehand plays the deuce side, the best way to get him to use his forehand is to serve a lot of balls to that side, which I suspect will not be the case, or for him to run around his backhand, in which case he is hitting an emergency-type forehand. It is easier for him to run around his backhand when returning in the ad court.

The most difficult shot in doubles in terms of execution is the inside-out crosscourt backhand return by a right-hander in the deuce court. If one person does that better than the other, then that person should play the forehand side.

Most people think the left-hander should go in the backhand court. But not necessarily. Let's face it, except for service returns, most balls are going to go down the middle, where doubles strategists tell you to hit it. That means forehands down the middle, which means putting the lefty in the deuce court.

Remember, when you start a new set you can change the

serving order and the receiving sides. But you cannot do either within a set.

Seven Suggestions on Doubles Tactics and Teamwork

1. I sometimes think this motto should be engraved on the racquet handle of every doubles player: "Get your first serve in." Do not give your opponents the opportunity to tee off on the return of your second serve.

2. Tennis is a game of position, and the dominant position in doubles is at the net. If you don't develop some facility for going to the net, you are forever relegating yourself to a low level of doubles prowess. No great doubles team on any level wins a lot of tournaments playing at the baseline. You need to go in and knock off points with volleys. Your choice of equipment can contribute to your volleying consistency. If you specialize in doubles, use a widebody racquet. If you just hold it tight and aim it where you would like the ball to go, the racquet will do the rest. You can volley quite effectively with little racquet-head motion, which is key during rapid doubles exchanges.

3. The overhead is a key barometer of confidence in a doubles match. If you miss one, you are liable to miss several, and your opponents will exploit that weakness with a flood of lobs. Get your racquet up early on the overhead so you have time to make the shot.

4. The trend in modern men's pro doubles is to blast away, beginning on the return of serve. It probably started with

John McEnroe and Peter Fleming, one of the doubles teams on the Davis Cup teams I captained. They both had big serves, so they would crush their returns until they got hot and strung a series of them together for a break. But recreational players who do that make too many errors (and probably don't hold serve as easily as McEnroe and Fleming did). You should rely more on placement than on power. Use two or three shots to split your opponents, then finish with a putaway into the hole.

5. A basic tenet of good doubles is to go down the middle when in doubt. But also remember that the court is an extra four and a half feet wide in each alley. So mix in the occasional down-the-line return to keep the net player honest, and use soft crosscourt angles during rallies to split your opponents and then go between them for the winner.

6. A mutual understanding between the two players is critical to a doubles team's success. You need to develop chemistry and trust, so that when one player makes a comment or suggestion during a match, he knows his partner won't take offense. It's important to communicate with your partner during points, between points, and between games.

The most common communication is a call of "Mine!" when covering a ball hit between the two of you. Sometimes your conversation between points and games will just be verbal encouragement. If one member of the team is playing badly, the other must compensate and provide support until his teammate recovers his game. Good teams play well even when one member is not at his best.

Other times your communication will involve tactics. Another of our Davis Cup doubles teams was Stan Smith and Bob Lutz. (I played Davis Cup with them in the late '60s and early '70s, then served as their captain in the early '80s.) Smith might tell Lutz that he was going to run around his backhand to hit a big forehand return, so Lutz would be looking for an opportunity to poach on their opponents' first volley. Another pair who played on teams I captained, Ken Flach and Robert Seguso, used signals before each serve. The netman gave a behind-the-back signal to the server to indicate where he wanted the ball to go. That did two things. First, it removed any doubt about the service target, which especially helped in tight spots where decisiveness was imperative. Second, it forced Flach and Seguso to think before each point, to focus on exactly what they wanted to do.

7. Challenge your opponents with different formations. The Australian formation, where the net player lines up on the same side as the receiver, is a good way to counter a team with good crosscourt returns; the unorthodox look makes them hit the shot they don't want to hit. The "I" formation, in which the net player crouches down while straddling the center service line, became a favorite on the women's tour in the early '90s. It intimidates opponents because they don't know which way the net person is going to move. Of course, the "I" only works if you tell your partner which way you *are* going to go.

When to Stay Back in Doubles

When serving, one player up at the net and one back at the baseline is better than both back, although you do see that at some low levels of club doubles because one of the partners is simply afraid to be at the net. But when you are receiving, on some occasions it is better to begin with both players back.

A basic advantage is you can survey the entire point as it is being played without having to turn around. Of course, staying back invites the serving team, which already has the positioning advantage, to close in and knock the point off at the net.

One tactical reason for having both players on the receiving team stay back is if one of you has lost confidence in your return of serve and you don't want to expose your partner to bullets in the chest from the server's netman as he poaches.

Another is to use the lob.

A third is to change your opponents' perspective. If you have been playing one up and one back for a set and a half, and all of a sudden both players pull back to the baseline, you force your opponents to think a little. They cannot react instinctively because they don't know what you are going to do: are you going to lob, chip the return and both charge in, or unleash a barrage of topspin ground strokes aimed at passing your opponents, making them play low balls or simply frustrating them into an error with your consistency? When both receivers drop back, it changes the server's perception of his target quite a bit. It may make him try a bigger first serve than he normally would. Then, when he misses it, the receiver's partner might step forward again for the second serve. All of that variation changes the pace and tempo and keeps your opponents guessing.

If you are the serving team, a counterplay against a team that is staying back is to purposely volley short in order to bring one player up and, thus, open the court. Usually the player who runs up will opt for a safe shot down the middle, which you can cover and volley back between him and his partner.

Partnership Dynamics in Doubles

Personal compatibility is key to a lasting partnership. It is no longer the dictatorship of singles but a small oligarchy. You are talking about a committee of two deciding everything. No matter what, though, in most teams there is one player who has a stronger personality than the other—John Newcombe rather than Tony Roche, John McEnroe rather than Peter Fleming. Meaning that if there were two different views of what to do, McEnroe was going to break the tie and Fleming was going to accede to that.

For those great teams, along with Bob Hewitt and Frew McMillan, Stan Smith and Bob Lutz, and, on a more local level, the longtime northern California pair of Hugh Ditzler and Clif Mayne, the idea of splitting up didn't enter their minds. They felt that they could work out whatever was bothering them.

The first telltale sign that a breakup is coming is an increased irritation at your partner's mistakes. You really want to minimize, or cut out entirely if at all possible, any on-court altercations between the two partners. It is not unforgivable, but it is not a good thing. Not only does it deepen the fissures in your current partnership, but also, as word gets around, no one else will want to play with you for fear that you will try to embarrass them on the court.

A legitimate reason to split is if the two of you started playing doubles at a relatively inexperienced skill level and one has progressed much faster than the other. The one who improves faster is going to want to find another partner who will allow him to step up a level.

Try making some changes before you break up. If you start losing a lot, it simply may be because the partner playing the forehand court should be playing the backhand court. Teams as great as Smith and Lutz or Navratilova and Shriver occasionally changed receiving sides to reinvigorate the partnership.

When the U.S. Davis Cup pair of Rick Leach and Jim Pugh parted a few years ago, they explained that they had just gone stale. To me, that meant they could not work out their temporary personal incompatibility. It had nothing to do with lack of success, because they had had very good results.

Mixed Doubles

Playing mixed doubles with a mate has proven to be rather difficult. The couple/doubles team needs to set some ground rules, and you absolutely must stick to them. Decide that neither one is going to get too upset if the other one does not play as well as he or she can. That's the rule. Otherwise, it can get embarrassing out there. And usually it is the man who gets upset at the woman. And leave your disagreements on the tennis court, although that is difficult to do.

In a lot of social mixed doubles the woman stands meekly over by the singles sideline and the man, playing Mr. Macho, runs all over the place. It is sad to see. And if it happens, you know that team is not going to go very far. You cannot win good doubles that way.

Mixed doubles can be a lot more fun than it has been portrayed. It would have been interesting to see Boris Becker and Steffi Graf play against John McEnroe and Martina Navratilova in their prime.

Team Tennis

Playing for a team is a good way to get started in competitive tennis. The U.S. Tennis Association has a huge league program. Then there's Billie Jean King's World TeamTennis. And a couple of cities, Atlanta and Minneapolis–St. Paul, have incredibly well-organized league competitions.

I played a lot of team tennis when I was a kid. I grew up and played at Brookfield Playground in Richmond, Virginia, and we played against Clark Spring and Armstrong and Oakwood playgrounds. Those matches were big deals; you always thought the other parks were better for some reason.

The ultimate team experience for me was Davis Cup, first as a player and later as captain of the U.S. team. It is a unique experience for several reasons. First, coaching by the captain is allowed during matches; it is against the rules in regular tournaments. Second, you build a sense of camaraderie with your teammates that normally isn't there. Only in Davis Cup will you see tennis pros cheering loudly for each other. Third, Davis Cup brings out the best in players. They are inspired because they are playing not just for themselves but for their teammates and their country. They are treated like heroes when they win. That is why Davis Cup has produced stunning upsets that you seldom see in tournament tennis. For me, the Davis Cup team feeling was an unusual and unbeatable part of tennis.

Senior Tennis

The largest-growing segment of the tennis-playing public is seniors. There are a few factors that make tennis a good sport for seniors. One is that you can make up for a loss of brawn by using your brain on the court. That is why the drop shot and the lob are used so effectively by older players. Another is that today's more powerful, widebody racquets have given older players a new lease on life in the same way that large-headed drivers have helped golfers such as Jack Nicklaus keep up with their long-driving younger colleagues. (I recommend that seniors use a full oversize model even if it isn't a widebody.) They make it easier to hit the ball with some pace. A third is that tennis has doubles as well as singles, so when you begin to lose your mobility, you can still play and have fun without worrying as much about court coverage.

In terms of strategy, you should make one major adjustment. The first two points of receiving games are critical for older players. If you get up 0–15 or 0–30, be ready to work hard, and if you extend that lead to 0–40, 15–40, 30–40, or ad out, go all out for the break. But when you fall way behind on your opponent's serve, avoid an extended rally to save energy. Kiss the game off and wait for your next opportunity.

On the competitive side, the USTA runs annual national championships on all four surfaces and ranks players in age categories up to eighty-five-and-over. In fact, tournament tennis is one activity in which you benefit from getting older—every five years you are among the youngest players in your age bracket. Without question, the greatest senior player of all time is Dorothy "Dodo" Cheney of Santa Monica, Calif., who now is in her seventies. She has won more than two hundred U.S. national championships, almost all of them in the senior age groups beginning with the women's forty-and-over.

How to Play a Tournament

Competing in a big tournament away from home imposes pressures and problems for players at all levels. Even if it is not Wimbledon or the U.S. Open, the experience is no less significant to you as a player. So you have to be prepared. Here are some guidelines; some may seem like common sense, but it is not unusual to overlook the obvious when you get caught up in the excitement of the event.

Check ahead with the tournament organizers to learn what

surface you will be playing on and what brand and type of balls will be used. Then practice at home on a similar court with the same balls. If you can, arrive at the tournament site a day early to practice there. And try to practice every day of a multi-day event. You will have no difficulty finding practice partners if you are the smart one who books a practice court the day before.

Be sure you take enough equipment to get you comfortably through the event. You need at least two racquets and a few sets of the string you prefer. You probably can get a racquet strung at the tournament, but the stringer may not have the string you like or the string job may not be exactly to your taste, so have a backup racquet or two. Also take plenty of clothes and at least two pairs of broken-in tennis shoes. The last thing you need is to get blisters from new shoes halfway through the tournament.

Check out the transportation details—especially precise directions to the courts and information about local traffic conditions. There is no point in traveling a long way and then being defaulted for being late.

Find out the precise time of your match the day before, and then organize your daily routine around that time. For example, if you have a morning match at eleven o'clock, get up early and go right out and practice for forty-five minutes. Then take a shower and have breakfast. Don't eat a heavy meal; stick to juice, cereal, toast, and fruit. Get to the courts an hour ahead of your match time and relax by taking in the tournament scene or shooting the breeze with other players in the locker room.

Work out a game plan. If you have never seen your opponent play, stick to a strategy that has worked for you in the past and give it a chance to work. Several games may go by before a pattern emerges that requires a shift in your plan.

Never assume that you have to play out of your mind to beat a seeded player. Tennis history is littered with early-round upsets. When an unknown beats a seed, it is usually because the unknown plays steady tennis while the seed makes more mistakes than usual. So if you meet a favorite, concentrate on getting the ball back and letting him make the errors. But if the flow of the match goes your way, be a little more decisive than usual and pour on the pressure. If you give a top player too many chances, he may find his game and turn the match around.

Conversely, if you are seeded, never underestimate an opponent. Some teenage hotshot may beat the pants off you if you become complacent about your own ability.

Finally, if you are likely to lose early in singles, by all means play doubles, too. You will have more fun, you will gain valuable experience, and you might surprise yourself by doing well.

How to Watch a Tournament

To get the most out of following a big pro tournament in person or on television, the first thing you need is a draw sheet. Almost every major newspaper now prints the singles draws of the Grand Slam events on the eve of the tournaments. Cut it out and copy it in order—from the first player at the top to the 128th player at the bottom. Once you have the match-ups in front of you, keep track of the action by filling in the winners' names and the scores each day. Then you will be able to anticipate the most interesting upcoming matches.

In the early rounds, focus on potential stars of tomorrow. For instance, you might pay attention to the results of the U.S. and Wimbledon junior champions or the NCAA winners. Two things to look for in assessing the long-term potential of young players are their court coverage and their returns of serve. If they are quick and have steady returns, they may go far. Also, follow the results of rookie pros who have had good results during the year. They could do some damage against higher-ranked players. Take note of their strengths and weaknesses, which shots they seem afraid to hit, how they react to pressure stages of a match, and how well they close out a match when they get ahead.

In the middle rounds, start looking for upsets. One way to anticipate an upset is to consider how comfortable a seeded player is on the tournament surface. For example, a high-seeded clay-courter at Wimbledon is a fish out of water on the grass courts there. Often what looks like an upset on paper would have been no surprise if you had taken a poll of players in the locker room before the match.

When the seeds begin facing each other in the round of sixteen, watch for historically tough rivalries. Usually those players have played each other many times. There are certain players who always prove to be tough for the favorites. Because of past success against a higher seed, such a player is not scared of his opponent, and the higher-ranked player is wary going into the match. A confrontation like that is a match worth watching, even if the favorite wins.

There are two types of pressure at the big events—the pressure of getting to the final and the pressure of playing in it. Just reaching the final gets your name in the record books. But once you get there, the pressure to win is huge. Having won the tournament before is a big help—past champions may feel more confident. To me, the player who has had a tougher time reaching the final has an edge because he is match tough, while his opponent could be a bit overconfident. A long match in the semis won't have a great effect unless the final is a marathon, too. The player who is better able to handle the pressure of being in the final has the advantage going into the match.

Finally, if you have been watching on television, go right out and play as soon as the match is over. You will be pumped up from the fun of watching such talented, exciting players. You will still be turned on by what you saw when you get to the courts, and you may play better than usual.

Television Talk

Tennis on television has contributed immeasurably to the growth and success of the sport worldwide. Wimbledon is watched by 400 million viewers in more than seventy countries. All of us who have done match commentary have been accused of talking too much.

There are two general approaches to how much explaining

is attempted between points. The first theory is that tennis on the networks—ABC, NBC, CBS—has such low ratings relative to, say, football, that the nuances of the game need to be reviewed. Although viewers don't know it, the producers of the program feed subjects for possible comment and prod the announcers to pursue a particular line of conversation. More often than not, it is these network producers who abhor too much of a voice void.

The second approach is more common to cable telecasts and the BBC at Wimbledon. The theory here is that since the households watching had to pay for the service, the viewer is assumed to be knowledgeable. Hence, the announcers can talk less.

Another reason some of us talk too much is that we are plied with so much statistical information about what is happening during a match and how it may relate to past matches, surfaces, and opponents. We may say more because there is so much more that we can say than we could five years ago. The IBM Matchfacts system now being used at ATP Tour events, for example, provides about two hundred different statistical categories and historical facts at our disposal with no more than three keystrokes.

I've had a long connection with computers (I attended the U.S. Army's Data Processing School at Fort Harrison, Indiana, back in 1967), so I find the possibilities of their use in covering tennis on television fascinating and challenging. In truth, we are still sorting it out and learning to pare down the stats to what is most important for the match involved. All us analysts—such as Billie Jean King, Mary Carillo, Bud Collins,

Chris Evert, John McEnroe, Fred Stolle, Tony Trabert—caucus with our statisticians before the day's matches and decide which facts are most important. I always ask them, "What is the most relevant category and number that may decide the outcome?" I may use their answer in my opening comments at the beginning of a show.

The tendency, though, is to make for lazier analysts since the computer can always keep us up-to-date. The view I attempt to offer as a commentator is based on not only what I consider the relevant statistics but also my own hunches derived from having played the game on the professional level. After all, that is what they pay us experts for—our expert opinions.

Widebody Racquets

A widebody—a racquet whose frame is thick when viewed from the side—makes certain shots easier. If you keep your stroke simple, there is no question that the widebody makes the volley easier. You only have to stick your racquet out there, hold on tight, and let the racquet do the work. And it certainly helps the backhand: the inherent power in the racquet makes up for the physical weakness in the backhand grip.

Conversely, a widebody may hurt you on the forehand and serve because the racquet does so much of the work, and if you don't have great feel for control in your hands, you may be holding a loose cannon. I believe that any time you use a more powerful racquet, whether it is a widebody or simply an oversize-head model of conventional frame width, you should strive for a smoother stroke to enhance your control of that power. With a widebody, that smooth swing also should be compact. Intermediate club players who poke at the ball will poke it a little harder with a widebody. While widebody racquets are responsible for a breakthrough in power, in my book the key to improvement is not hitting the ball harder, but hitting the ball more squarely and more consistently in the sweetspot.

Despite the almost universal switch to widebodies among club players, you don't see male pros rushing to use them. Pete Sampras, Jim Courier, Stefan Edberg, Michael Stich, Boris Becker, Goran Ivanisevic—all of them use conventional-width frames. They don't need more power, they need more control. They also prefer a racquet that allows them to swing at the ball with a full, long stroke, rather than a racquet that does the work for them. Finally, because they swing on such a violent, vertical arc for topspin, they might catch more balls on the wide lip of the hoop in a widebody.

Thus I cannot blame widebodies for the trend to boring power tennis in the men's pro game. I can blame other changes in racquet technology, though. Along with larger head sizes, space-age technology has made racquets more powerful, too, especially in the hands of male pros. The trend is exacerbated on fast grass courts. The men's singles at Wimbledon in 1991 was the dullest I had watched in a long time; statistics from the final between Stich and Becker showed that the average length of points was less than three seconds and that the ball was in play only three minutes and forty-two seconds of each hour of match time.

On the other hand, I agree with those who say that wide-bodies have helped women's pro tennis as a spectator sport because the players are hitting the ball harder. That is especially true of matches on clay, where, with the exception of the occasional compelling match, such as the 1985 French Open final between Chris Evert and Martina Navratilova, women's tennis was a succession of boring, slow-paced baseline rallies, one after another.

Strings

Pros will string racquets differently for different atmospheric conditions. If they are playing at high noon in sunny, dry Scottsdale, Arizona, they will string them tighter. But if they are playing the fourth match on Court 1 at Wimbledon late on a cool, overcast London afternoon, they will drop their tension.

Weather and humidity aside, the basic rule to follow is: string looser for more power (from trampolining, not immediate power from the frame itself) and string tighter for control. If you play regularly, you ought to have your racquet restrung as many times in a year as you play in a week. Even if strings don't break, they will lose their tension and resiliency over time. Also, have the same stringer string your racquet each time on the same machine for consistency.

If you ever get to sit close to the court for a pro match, you can determine which player has the tighter string tension just by listening. The sharper, crisper ping indicates tighter tension, while a duller thud indicates looser tension. When a pro breaks a string, you often see him or her tapping his or her palm against the strings of two replacement racquets to check their relative tensions before picking one. A string doesn't always break on court, though. I've been on airplane flights with my playing colleagues when all of a sudden there was a popping sound from the overhead compartment where we had stashed our racquets. A string had broken, usually in a big-headed racquet.

Shoes

If you play a lot, shoes are probably, along with racquets, the most important purchase you are going to make. And the shoe technology is so good now that certainly there is a brand and model that will serve you best, whether you have long narrow feet or short wide feet, whether you have flat feet or high arches. The price of those shoes could range from $60 to $150, although a lot of extra money in high-priced models goes to styling. Some expensive shoes have a lot of different pieces on them that serve no function at all except to differentiate them from all other shoes.

Regardless of the technology, the first thing to do is to get a shoe that fits right.

If you are really serious, I recommend getting your feet checked out at your local sports medicine or sports podiatry clinic before you buy shoes. A doctor may even prescribe custom orthotics, or insoles, for your feet. (Be sure to take them with you when shopping for new shoes so that you get a good fit.)

Why is all this so important? If you are wearing shoes that are worn out or are the wrong fit, you can suffer injuries far away from your feet. You can wind up with ankle problems, knee problems, hip problems, or back problems. A serious player should realize that part of the expense of playing tennis is keeping his or her feet properly shod.

The Pros' Big Duffel Bags

What is in those duffel bags? A lot: up to a dozen or more racquets, string, grips, lead tape, string stencils and ink, shirts, shorts, skirts, shoes, warm-up suits, sweatbands, hats, sunscreen, elastic bandages, bananas, candy, water, sports drinks, makeup, hair spray, wallets, purses, jump ropes, balls, instruction notes. It is quite a change from Bill Tilden's day, when he would walk onto the court in a big woolly cardigan sweater carrying nothing more than four uncovered racquets with bare wood handles.

Of course, there is a commercial side to those bags, too. Racquet or clothing companies require their contract players to carry them. They are paying the players for the exposure. That's why they construct the bags so that they will sit upright instead of collapsing at the ends. And they will instruct the players to set the bags on the court at a certain angle so that when television focuses on the player during a change-over, the company logo is pointing right at the camera.

Have Racquet, Will Travel

If you are a serious recreational player, take your racquet when you go on a trip. There are places to play almost everywhere you go. Before you leave, check with your credit card company's leisure services division to see if it has a program to help traveling players find games. In the Sun Belt, most hotels have courts. And many of the country's big-city downtown hotels have playing privileges for their guests at area clubs. In San Francisco, for instance, you should check with the concierge to see if the hotel has privileges at the San Francisco Tennis Club, an indoor facility. Or you can go out to Golden Gate Park, one of the top public tennis centers in America. If you are a member of a USTA club, don't be shy about calling a local club to ask if they have any reciprocal privileges.

As a pro, I never checked my racquets for air travel. I could not afford to lose them, so I always carried them on board, and I suggest that you do the same. Racquet companies have made it easy and convenient to do so with today's racquet cases. And just to be on the safe side, pack all-white clothes because you never know when a club may have a slightly more restrictive dress code than you are used to. You can never go wrong with all white.

Conflicting Advice

Taking a lesson is a good idea when you are on vacation. It is a good way to get some exercise and it may give you the chance to play on an unfamiliar surface. One potential problem may arise, though. When I do holiday clinics at the Doral in Miami, it is inevitable that at least one student will tell me that I am contradicting the instruction he or she got from his or her home pro. I try to work around the difference, or simply say that while what the home pro says has a lot of merit, there is another way of looking at it. As a pupil, expect discrepancies. But don't get too worked up about it.

Tennis Camps

Going to tennis camp is a sensational idea, once you have progressed beyond the beginner level, as long as you are aware going in that such a vacation can be total tennis immersion. If you have never been to a tennis camp, you will hit more balls there in a given amount of time than ever before. It is a lot of fun, you meet a lot of people, and you see a lot of different styles.

But if you have never hit a tennis ball, my advice is don't go to a tennis camp. Too many people are going to be impatient with you. It is not an ideal place for beginners, who probably are better off starting with group lessons at a local club.

Certainly a trip to tennis camp will absorb your mind and take it away from your day job. And that is what vacations are for, to help you unwind. Think of going to tennis camp as part of the growing accent on "experience" vacations—such as going on archaeological digs—as opposed to just sitting on a beach reading a book and stuffing yourself with fattening foods.

I suggest you go with three specific goals uppermost in your mind: 1. to learn a new shot; 2. to work on your biggest weakness; and 3. to make some new lifelong friends.

Each camp has a different philosophy of what it thinks is important instruction. Wherever you go, though, there is no question you should leave camp with your game better off than when you started. The tennis-camp business requires a lot of attention to detail. While I enjoy the teaching experience, I was never that interested in running a camp. If you decide to go to a camp that advertises instruction by big-name players or coaches, be sure to ask when they will appear and how much on-court teaching you will receive directly from them.

Tennis Parents

The phrase "tennis parent" is a variation of the more generic and widely known "Little League parent." I understand from experts such as Jim Loehr, a pioneer in coaching the mental side of tennis, that there is a relatively precise definition of "Little League parent" in the annals of sports psychology. Little League parents are parents/guardians who generally 1. have an inflated opinion of their child's athletic skills; 2. believe that their child and they themselves are not receiving fair treatment; 3. treat competition at this entry level as if it were the World Series; and 4. are hypersensitive to any perceived slights. Another way of putting it is that they are just not very realistic.

Here are a few guidelines to keep you from becoming a "tennis parent."

First, be supportive. The presence of a parent at practice sessions or at tournaments is a plus, if done right. My wife, Jeanne, goes to our daughter Camera's ballet class and some other activities. Parental support is good whether at a child's practice or play, as long as you provide it without putting undue pressure on him or her.

Second, come to some sort of informal contract with everyone who has a responsibility for your child's instruction. Do not interfere with what the pro is trying to impart to your child. And be realistic about asking why your child is not in an advanced class.

Third, be consistent and prompt in responding to bad behavior. Set ground rules before your child even starts. A child should know what's going to happen if he or she does X. And when X happens, punishment has to be swift and sure and consistent. It is very important that there be little time lost between the incident and the penalty. Establish a set of expectations, discuss why they are the way they are, and do not allow for any excuses. This consistency will convince the child that his or her behavior is wrong.

In a tournament setting, if your child's behavior reaches a certain egregious level, it is your moral duty to go out there and stop the match. I certainly would do it. I threw my racquet once on the courts at Brookfield Playground in Richmond. My father came out the door of our house, which was adjacent to the courts, to get me the instant it happened. I did not play again for a long time. I was grounded. I never threw my racquet again, either.

Fourth, never accept cheating. Kids will cheat guiltlessly if you do not seriously condemn it. Most juniors who play tournaments at an early age do not have an umpire. They call their own lines. I think this process is a good exercise in self-restraint and self-control. When two ten-year-olds are playing a tennis match, a hell of a lot more is being taught, and a lot more is at stake, than winning or losing the match. They are learning values and attitudes.

A kid who comes off the court victorious after having cheated at age ten is worse off than the opponent who stuck to his or her moral system and lost. The parent or guardian who brought the losing player to the tournament must reinforce that after the match is over by saying, "You lost the match, but I'm very proud of the way you conducted yourself."

If your child wins a match and you saw that he or she cheated but no one else saw it and he got away with it, you've got to tell him when he gets off the court. You've got to say, "I don't want you to do that anymore."

One of the most difficult dilemmas for the child to be in is when he or she says, "Yeah, I cheated, but he cheated me first." If it is true that the child's opponent started the cheating, then according to his moral code it is OK to cheat back.

He doesn't look at it as having lowered himself to his opponent's level; he sees it as righteous retribution for having been wronged. It is very difficult to convince the child otherwise, especially if he comes off the court having lost.

Remember, there is no question that the kids—and their parents—who cheat are widely known. Everybody knows who they are and knows they will do it again.

Fifth, never reprimand your child in public about the outcome of a match. Whether or not the child has won or lost a tennis match is almost insignificant in his or her overall upbringing.

Sixth, under no circumstances should you talk, scream, or yell at your child's opponent. If you have a complaint about how your child's opponent is behaving, if he is cheating or whatever, speak to a qualified person in authority, such as the referee or the tournament director.

Prodigies and School

Mary Joe Fernandez stayed in high school and graduated with her class even as she was competing on the pro tour as a world-class top-ten player. She was an honors student. It was not a mistake in the least. I thought it was very commendable. I don't think she lost a thing, tenniswise, I really don't. She has maintained some balance in her life and gained some maturity. Those two things have not hurt her tennis.

You have got to look at the long run. The question to ask is not, "How will concentrating too much on the books hurt my junior tennis career?" That is too shortsighted. The question is, "How will it affect the rest of my life, with all the other possibilities therein, if I play junior tennis or college tennis or pro tennis or if I don't play pro tennis?"

Let me put it this way: making sure your schoolwork is not neglected is a high-percentage play. It is a very high-percentage play.

A Note About the Authors

ARTHUR ASHE won the men's singles titles at Wimbledon in 1975, the U.S. Open in 1968, and the Australian Open in 1970. He was a finalist in Grand Slam tournaments four other times. He was ranked No. 1 in the world in 1968 (sharing the No. 1 position with Rod Laver) and in 1975. Among his other major singles victories were the 1975 WCT Finals, the 1967 U.S. Clay Courts, the 1967 U.S. Hard Courts, and the 1965 NCAAs. In doubles, he won the French Open and Australian Open titles and was a finalist at Wimbledon and the U.S. Open. In all, he won thirty-three pro singles titles and eighteen pro doubles titles. An eleven-time member of the U.S. Davis Cup team, he played on championship squads in 1963, 1968, 1969, 1970, and 1978. During a five-year reign as captain, he led the U.S. Davis Cup team to victory in 1981 and 1982. In 1985, he was inducted into the International Tennis Hall of Fame. In addition to his competitive career, he served as the international director of tennis at the Doral Resort and Country Club in Miami, Florida, an analyst on ABC's and HBO's tennis telecasts, and an instruction editor of *Tennis* magazine. He was a founder or co-founder of several community-service organizations—among them the National Junior Tennis League, the ABC Cities Program, the Athlete-Career Connection, and the Safe Passage Foundation—that introduced young people to tennis and that used tennis as a way to help young people pursue their education and career goals.

ALEXANDER MCNAB served from 1986 to 1990 as Editor of *Tennis* magazine, where he now is a Contributing Editor. He collaborated with Arthur Ashe on Ashe's instruction articles for the magazine from 1982 until 1993. He is the author of *The Tennis Doctor*.

A Note on the Type

The text of this book was set in Simoncini Garamond, a modern version by Francesco Simoncini of the type attributed to the famous Parisian type cutter Claude Garamond (ca. 1480–1561). Garamond was a pupil of Geoffroy Tory and is believed to have based his letters on the Venetian models, although he introduced a number of important differences, and it is to him we owe the letter that we know as old style. He gave to his letters a certain elegance and a feeling of movement that won for their creator an immediate reputation and the patronage of Francis I of France.

Composed by American-Stratford Graphic Services, Inc.,
Brattleboro, Vermont
Printed and bound by The Haddon Craftsmen,
Scranton, Pennsylvania
Designed by Anthea Lingeman